THE LANE
THAT HAD NO
TURNING

Sir Gilbert Parker
(photograph by Pirie MacDonald)

THE LANE
THAT HAD NO
TURNING

AND OTHER TALES
CONCERNING THE PEOPLE OF PONTIAC

GILBERT PARKER

Rock's Mills Press
Oakville, Ontario

PUBLISHED BY
Rock's Mills Press

Copyright © 2015 Rock's Mills Press
Introduction © 2015 Jen Rubio
Book Layout © 2013 BookDesignTemplates.com
ALL RIGHTS RESERVED

The Lane That Had No Turning was first published by Doubleday, Page & Company in 1900 and in Canada by George N. Morang & Co. Ltd. the same year. This edition follows the Morang edition, with the omission of the dedication and of the final section of nine short stories that were included under the umbrella title "Parables of a Province."

Library and Archives Canada cataloguing in publication data is available from the publisher by email at customer.service@rocksmillspress.com.

Cover image: Tony Collins

FIRST EDITION
ISBN-13: 978-0-988-1293-7-5

Contents

Introduction *by Jen Rubio*		*vii*
The Lane That Had No Turning		*1*
	1. The Return of Madelinette	*1*
	2. When the Red-Coats Came	*12*
	3. Man to Man and Steel to Steel	*23*
	4. Madelinette Makes a Discovery	*34*
	5. What Will She Do With It?	*38*
	6. The One Who Saw	*42*
	7. The Pursuit	*48*
	8. Face to Face	*57*
	9. The Biter Bitten	*68*
	10. The Door That Would Not Open	*71*
The Absurd Romance of P'tite Louison		*87*
The Little Bell of Honour		*94*
A Son of the Wilderness		*117*
A Worker in Stone		*124*
The Tragic Comedy of Annette		*136*
The Marriage of the Miller		*140*
Mathurin		*144*
The Story of the Lime Burner		*152*
The Woodsman's Story of the Great White Chief		*160*
Uncle Jim		*164*
The House with the Tall Porch		*174*
Parpon the Dwarf		*179*
Times Were Hard in Pontiac		*201*
Medallion's Whim		*207*
The Prisoner		*220*
An Upset Price		*226*
A Fragment of Lives		*235*
The Man That Died at Alma		*240*
The Baron of Beaugard		*252*
A Note on the Text and Author		*265*

Introduction

This is a decidedly strange collection of short fiction about early French Canada by a wealthy, English-speaking, globe-trotting politician from Ontario. Parker had become one of the world's best-selling authors in 1896 with his novel about the conquest of Quebec, *The Seats of the Mighty*. He returned in 1900 to writing about Canada, this time fictionalizing a mythic village in rural Quebec called Pontiac in *The Lane That Had No Turning*.

Critics have, by and large, steered well clear of Gilbert Parker, aside from occasional expressions of disapproval. And on many counts Parker is a critical conundrum. His stories were not written for Canadians but sold successfully—rather too successfully—to British and American popular periodicals. In this collection the stories are at best stereotypical misrepresentations of salt-of-the-earth "peasant" life in what is now Quebec. They verge on an authenticity hoax, an "invented tradition" pulled over the eyes of an unenlightened, credulous readership a century ago. (Parker claimed in one of the prefaces to his collected works that these were realistic depictions of French Canadian life. They are in fact the stuff of a very vivid imagination.)

The problems don't end here. These treacherously readable, delightfully hair-raising, and occasionally gruesome stories portray French Canadians as picturesque, backwards, superstitious, and tradition-bound in a way that makes modern English Canadians cringe. Parker dramatizes genuine issues—French Canadian nationalism and ethnic conflict for example—as matters of historical romance. And there is a whiff of intellectual evasion in Parker's fiction. He did not tangle with the more difficult contemporary issues of realism or naturalism in literature when he might have done so; he simply excused himself with the statement that, for him, art was there to bring pleasure. In his stories, music and song are treated as the real human achievements.

If anything these stories might fall into the category of fin-de-siècle Gothic, published as they are around the time of George du Maurier's *Trilby* (1895), Bram Stoker's *Dracula* (1897), and Henry James' *The Turn of the Screw* (1898). Parker's tales are at times downright weird, with dark intrigue, degenerate hearts, tortured souls, and desperate violence. They contain an occasional *frisson* from the literature of France: a hunchback coupled with a beautiful young singer, a dwarf kissing a young girl's corpse, a liberal sprinkling of unrefined *blasphèmes*.

How, then, should we explain the great success of these stories? Parker was considered by some to be one of the best writers in the English language at the turn of the century. The truth is his writing is full of humanity and compassion. It is compelling and enjoyable, with colour, pathos, humour, sentimentality, occasional horror, and much charity. Perhaps our discomfort with Parker's fiction—stories that now seem to tread so uneasily in the no-man's land of authenticity, history, ethnicity, and cultural memory—is precisely where they become interesting.

—Jen Rubio
Hamilton, Ontario

THE LANE THAT HAD NO TURNING

THE LANE THAT HAD NO TURNING

CHAPTER ONE

The Return of
Madelinette

His Excellency the Governor—the English Governor of French Canada—was come to Pontiac, accompanied by a goodly retinue; by private secretary, military secretary, aide-de-camp, cabinet minister, and all that. He was making a tour of the Province, but it was obvious that he had gone out of his way to visit Pontiac, for there were disquieting rumours in the air concerning the loyalty of the district. Indeed, the Governor had arrived but twenty-four hours after a meeting had been held under the presidency of the

Seigneur,[1] at which resolutions easily translatable into sedition were presented. The Curé[2] and the Avocat,[3] arriving in the nick of time, had both spoken against these resolutions; with the result that the newborn ardour in the minds of the simple habitants had died down, and the Seigneur had parted from the Curé and the Avocat in anger.

Pontiac had been involved in an illegal demonstration once before. Valmond, the bizarre but popular Napoleonic pretender, had raised his standard there; the stones before the parish church had been stained with his blood; and he lay in the churchyard of St. Saviour's forgiven and unforgotten. How was it possible for Pontiac to forget him? Had he not left his little fortune to the parish? and had he not also left twenty thousand francs for the musical education of Madelinette Lajeunesse, the daughter of the village forgeron,[4] to learn singing of the best masters in Paris? Pontiac's wrong-doings had brought it more profit than penalty, more praise than punishment: for, after five years in France in the care of the Little Chemist's widow, Madelinette Lajeunesse had become the greatest singer of her day. But what had put the severest strain upon the modesty of Pontiac was the fact that, on the morrow of Madelinette's first triumph in Paris, she had married M. Louis Racine, the new Seigneur of Pontiac.

What more could Pontiac wish? It had been rewarded for its mistakes; it had not even been chastened, save that it was marked "Suspicious" as to its loyalty, at the headquarters of the English Government in Quebec. It should have worn a crown of thorns, but

---

[1] Early settlement patterns in New France (later Lower Canada; now Quebec) followed a semi-feudal tenure organization known as the seigneurial system; land was rented to farmers, or *habitants*, by the seigneur.

[2] Catholic priest.

[3] Lawyer.

[4] Blacksmith.

it flaunted a crown of roses. A most unreasonable good fortune seemed to pursue it. It had been led to expect that its new Seigneur would be an Englishman, one George Fournel, to whom, as the late Seigneur had more than once declared, the property was devised by will; but at his death no will had been found, and Louis Racine, the direct heir in blood, had succeeded to the property and the title.

Brilliant, enthusiastic, fanatically French, the new Seigneur had set himself to revive certain old traditions, customs, and privileges of the Seigneurial position. He was reactionary, seductive, generous, and at first he captivated the hearts of Pontiac. He did more than that. He captivated Madelinette Lajeunesse. In spite of her years in Paris—severe, studious years, which shut out the social world and the temptations of Bohemian life—Madelinette retained a strange simplicity of heart and mind, a desperate love for her old home which would not be gainsaid, a passionate loyalty to her past, which was an illusory attempt to arrest the inevitable changes that come with growth; and, with a sudden impulse, she had sealed herself to her past at the very outset of her great career by marriage with Louis Racine.

On the very day of their marriage Louis Racine had made a painful discovery. A heritage of his fathers, which had skipped two generations, suddenly appeared in himself: he was becoming a hunchback.

Terror, despair, gloom, anxiety had settled upon him. Three months later Madelinette had gone to Paris alone. The Seigneur had invented excuses for not accompanying her, so she went instead in the care of the Little Chemist's widow, as of old Louis had promised to follow within another three months, but had not done so. The surgical operation performed upon him was unsuccessful; the strange growth increased. Sensitive, fearful, and morose, he would not go to Europe to be known as the hunchback husband of Lajeunesse, the great singer. He dreaded the hour when Madelinette and he should meet again. A thousand times he pictured her as turning from him in loathing and contempt. He had married her because he loved her, but he knew well enough that ten thousand other men could love her just as well, and be something more than a deformed Seigneur of an obscure manor in Quebec.

As his gloomy imagination pictured the future, when Madelinette should return and see him as he was and cease to love him—to build up his Seigneurial honour to an undue importance, to give his position a fictitious splendour, became a mania with him. No ruler of a Grand Duchy ever cherished his honour dearer or exacted homage more persistently than did Louis Racine in the Seigneury of Pontiac. Coincident with the increase of these futile extravagances was the increase of his fanatical patriotism, which at last found vent in seditious writings, agitations, the purchase of rifles, incitement to rebellion, and the formation of an armed, liveried troop of dependants at the Manor. On the very eve of the Governor's coming, despite the Curé's and the Avocat's warnings, he had held a patriotic meeting intended to foster a stubborn, if silent, disregard of the Governor's presence amongst them.

The speech of the Curé, who had given guarantee for the good behaviour of his people to the Government, had been so tinged with sorrowful appeal, had recalled to them so acutely the foolish demonstration which had ended in the death of Valmond; that the people had turned from the exasperated Seigneur with the fire of monomania in his eyes, and had left him alone in the hall, passionately protesting that the souls of Frenchmen were not in them.

Next day, upon the church, upon the Louis Quinze Hotel,[5] and elsewhere, the Union Jack flew—the British colours flaunted it in Pontiac with welcome to the Governor. But upon the Seigneury was another flag—it of the golden-lilies.[6] Within the Manor House M. Louis Racine sat in the great Seigneurial chair, returned from the gates of death. As he had come home from the futile public meeting, galloping through the streets and out upon the Seigneury road in the dusk, his horse had shied upon a bridge, where mischievous lads waylaid travellers with ghostly heads made of lighted candles in hollowed pumpkins, and horse and man had been plunged into the stream beneath. His faithful servant Havel had seen the accident and dragged his insensible master from the water.

Now the Seigneur sat in the great arm-chair glowering out upon the cheerful day. As he brooded, shaken and weak and bitter—all his thoughts were bitter now—a flash of scarlet, a glint of white plumes crossed his line of vision, disappeared, then again came into view, and horses' hoofs rang out on the hard road below. He started to his feet, but fell back again, so feeble was he, then rang the bell at his side with nervous insistence. A door opened quickly behind him, and his voice said imperiously:

"Quick, Havel—to the door. The Governor and his suite have come. Call Tardif, and have wine and cake brought at once. When the Governor enters, let Tardif stand at the door, and you beside my

---

[5] The hotel is named after Louis XV (1710–1774), the King of France from 1715 until his death. The implication is that English–French historical rivalries have been reproduced in the village of Pontiac.

[6] The fleur-de-lis, a stylized flower often associated with the French monarchy (and later the design on the flag of Quebec).

chair. Have the men-at-arms get into livery, and make a guard of honour for the Governor when he leaves. Their new rifles too—and let old Fashode wear his medal! See that Lucre is not filthy—ha! ha! very good. I must let the Governor hear that. Quick—quick, Havel. They are entering the grounds. Let the Manor bell be rung, and every one mustered. He shall see that to be a Seigneur is not an empty honour. I am something in the state, something by my own right." His lips moved restlessly; he frowned; his hands nervously clasped the arms of the chair. "Madelinette too shall see that I am to be reckoned with, that I am not a nobody. By God, then, but she shall see it!" he added, bringing his clasped hand down hard upon the wood.

There was a stir outside, a clanking of chains, a champing of bits, and the murmurs of the crowd who were gathering fast in the grounds. Presently the door was thrown open and Havel announced the Governor. Louis Racine got to his feet, but the Governor hastened forward, and, taking both his hands, forced him gently back into the chair.

"No, no, my dear Seigneur. You must not rise. This is no state visit, but a friendly call to offer congratulations on your happy escape, and to inquire how you are."

The Governor said his sentences easily, but he suddenly flushed and was embarrassed, for Louis Racine's deformity, of which he had not known—Pontiac kept its troubles to itself—stared him in the face; and he felt the Seigneur's eyes fastened on him with strange intensity.

"I have to thank your Excellency," the Seigneur said in a hasty nervous voice. "I fell on my shoulders—that saved me. If I had fallen on my head I should have been killed, no doubt. My shoulders saved me!" he added, with a petulant insistence in his voice, a morbid anxiety in his face.

"Most providential," responded the Governor. "It grieves me that it should have happened on the occasion of my visit. I missed the Seigneur's loyal public welcome. But I am happy," he continued, with smooth deliberation, "to have it here in this old Manor House, where other loyal French subjects of England have done honour to their Sovereign's representative."

"This place is sacred to hospitality and patriotism, your Excellency," said Louis Racine, nervousness passing from his voice and a curious hard look coming into his face.

The Governor was determined not to see the double meaning. "It is a privilege to hear you say so. I shall recall the fact to her Majesty's Government in the report I shall make upon my tour of the province. I have a feeling that the Queen's pleasure in the devotion of her distinguished French subjects may take some concrete form."

The Governor's suite looked at each other significantly, for never before in his journeys had his Excellency hinted so strongly that an honour might be conferred. Veiled as it was, it was still patent as the sun. Spots of colour shot into the Seigneur's cheeks. An honour from the young English Queen—that would mate with Madelinette's fame. After all, it was only his due. He suddenly found it hard to be consistent. His mind was in a whirl. The Governor continued:

"It must have given you great pleasure to know that at Windsor her Majesty has given tokens of honour to the famous singer, the wife of a notable French subject, who, while passionately eager to keep alive French sentiment, has, as we believe, a deep loyalty to England."

The Governor had said too much. He had thought to give the Seigneur an opportunity to recede from his seditious position there and then, and to win his future loyalty. M. Racine's situation had peril, and the Governor had here shown him the way of escape. But he had said one thing that drove Louis Racine mad. He had given him unknown information about his own wife. Louis did not know that Madelinette had been received by the Queen, or that she had received "tokens of honour." Wild with resentment, he saw in the Governor's words a consideration for himself based only on the fact that he was the husband of the great singer. He trembled to his feet.

At that moment there was a cheering outside—great cheering— but he did not heed it; he was scarcely aware of it. If it touched his understanding at all, it only meant to him a demonstration in honour of the Governor.

"Loyalty to the flag of England, your Excellency!" he said, in a hoarse acrid voice—"you speak of loyalty to us whose lives for two centuries—" He paused, for he heard a voice calling his name.

"Louis! Louis! Louis!"

The fierce words he had been about to utter died on his lips, his eyes stared at the open window, bewildered and even frightened.

"Louis! Louis!"

Now the voice was inside the house. He stood trembling, both hands grasping the arms of the chair. Every eye in the room was now turned towards the door. As it opened, the Seigneur sank back in the chair, a look of helpless misery, touched by a fierce pride, covering his face.

"Louis!"

It was Madelinette, who, disregarding the assembled company, ran forward to him and caught both his hands in hers.

"O Louis, I have heard of your accident, and—" she stopped suddenly short. The Governor turned away his head. Every person in the room did the same. For as she bent over him—she saw. She saw for the first time; for the first time knew!

A look of horrified amazement, of shrinking anguish, crossed over her face. He felt the lightning—like silence, he knew that she had seen; he struggled to his feet, staring fiercely at her.

That one torturing instant had taken all the colour from her face, but there was a strange brightness in her eyes, a new power in her bearing. She gently forced him into the seat again.

"You are not strong enough, Louis. You must be tranquil."

She turned now to the Governor. He made a sign to his suite, who, bowing, slowly left the room. "Permit me to welcome you to your native land again, Madame," he said. "You have won for it a distinction it could never have earned, and the world gives you many honours."

She was smiling and still, and with one hand clasping her husband's, she said:

"The honour I value most my native land has given me: I am lady of the Manor here, and wife of the Seigneur Racine."

Agitated triumph came upon Louis Racine's face; a weird painful vanity entered into him. He stood up beside his wife, as she turned and looked at him, showing not a sign that what she saw disturbed her.

"It is no mushroom honour to be Seigneur of Pontiac, your Excellency," he said, in a tone that jarred. "The barony[7] is two

---

[7] English equivalent of *seigneurie*.

hundred years old. By rights granted from the crown of France, I am Baron of Pontiac."

"I think England has not yet recognised the title," said the Governor suggestively, for he was here to make peace, and in the presence of this man, whose mental torture was extreme, he would not allow himself to be irritated.

"Our baronies have never been recognised," said the Seigneur harshly. "And yet we are asked to love the flag of England and—"

"And to show that we are too proud to ask for a right that none can take away," interposed Madelinette graciously and eagerly, as though to prevent Louis from saying what he intended. All at once she had had to order her life anew, to replace old thoughts by new ones. "We honour and obey the rulers of our land, and fly the English flag, and welcome the English Governor gladly when he comes to us—will your Excellency have some refreshment?" she added quickly, for she saw the cloud on the Seigneur's brow. "Louis," she added quickly, "will you—"

"I have ordered refreshment," said the Seigneur excitedly, the storm passing from his face, however. "Havel, Tardif—where are you, fellows!" He stamped his foot imperiously.

Havel entered with a tray of wine and glasses, followed by Tardif loaded with cakes and comfits, and set them on the table.

Ten minutes later the Governor took his leave. At the front door he stopped surprised, for a guard of honour of twenty men were drawn up. He turned to the Seigneur.

"What soldiers are these?" he asked.

"The Seigneury company, your Excellency," replied Louis.

"What uniform is it they wear?" he asked in an even tone, but with a black look in his eye, which did not escape Madelinette.

"The livery of the Barony of Pontiac," answered the Seigneur.

The Governor looked at them a moment without speaking. "It is French uniform of the time of Louis Quinze," he said. "Picturesque, but informal," he added.

He went over, and taking a carbine from one of the men, examined it. "Your carbines are not so unconventional and antique," he said meaningly, and with a frosty smile. "The compromise of the centuries—hein?" he added to the Curé, who, with the Avocat, was now looking on with some trepidation. "I am wondering if it is quite legal. It is charming to have such a guard of honour, but I am wondering—wondering—eh, monsieur l'avocat, is it legal?"

The Avocat made no reply, but the Curé's face was greatly troubled. The Seigneur's momentary placidity passed.

"I answer for their legality, your Excellency," he said, in a high, assertive voice.

"Of course, of course, you will answer for it," said the Governor, smiling enigmatically. He came forward and held out his hand to Madelinette.

"Madame, I shall remember your kindness, and I appreciate the simple honours done me here. Your arrival at the moment of my visit is a happy circumstance."

There was a meaning in his eye—not in his voice—which went straight to Madelinette's understanding. She murmured something in reply, and a moment afterwards the Governor, his suite, and the crowd were gone; and the men-at-arms—the fantastic body of men in their antique livery—armed with the latest modern weapons, had gone back to civic life again.

Inside the house once more, Madelinette laid her hand upon Louis' arm with a smile that wholly deceived him for a moment. He thought now that she must have known of his deformity before she came—the world was so full of tale-bearers—and no doubt had long since reconciled herself to the painful fact. She had shown no surprise, no shrinking. There had been only the one lightning instant in which he had felt a kind of suspension of her breath and being, but when he had looked her in the face, she was composed and smiling. After all his frightened anticipation the great moment had come and gone without tragedy. With satisfaction he looked in the mirror in the hall as they passed inside the house. He saw no reason to quarrel with his face. Was it possible that the deformity did not matter after all?

He felt Madelinette's hand on his arm. He turned and clasped her to his breast.

He did not notice that she kept her hands under her chin as he drew her to him, that she did not, as had been her wont, put them on his shoulders. He did not feel her shrink, and no one, seeing, could have said that she shrank from him in ever so little.

"How beautiful you are!" he said, as he looked into her face.

"How glad I am to be here again, and how tired I am, Louis!" she said. "I've driven thirty miles since daylight." She disengaged herself. "I am going to sleep now," she added. "I am going to turn the key in my door till evening. Please tell Madame Marie so, Louis."

Inside her room alone she flung herself on her bed in agony and despair.

"Louis—Oh, my God!" she cried, and sobbed and sobbed her strength away.

CHAPTER TWO

When the Red-Coats Came

A month later there was a sale of the household effects, the horses and general possessions of Medallion the auctioneer, who, though a Protestant and an Englishman, had, by his wits and goodness of heart, endeared himself to the parish. Therefore the notables among the habitants had gathered in his empty house for a last drink of good-fellowship—Muroc the charcoalman, Duclosse the mealman,[8] Bénoît the ne'er-do-weel, Gingras the one-eyed shoemaker, and a few others. They had drunk the health of Medallion, they had drunk the health of the Curé, and now Duclosse the mealman raised his glass. "Here's to—"

"Wait a minute, porridge-pot," cried Muroc. "The best man here should raise the glass first and say the votre santé. 'Tis M'sieu' Medallion should speak and sip now."

Medallion was half-sitting on the window-sill, abstractedly listening. He had been thinking that his ships were burned behind

---

[8] A dealer in meal, or grain.

13

him, and that in middle-age he was starting out to make another camp for himself in the world, all because of the new Seigneur of Pontiac. Time was when he had been successful here, but Louis Racine had changed all that. His hand was against the English, and he had brought a French auctioneer to Pontiac. Medallion might have divided the parish as to patronage, but he had other views.

So he was going. Madelinette had urged him to stay, but he had replied that it was too late. The harm was not to be undone.

As Muroc spoke, every one turned towards Medallion. He came over and filled a glass at the table, and raised it.

"I drink to Madelinette, daughter of that fine old puffing forgeron Lajeunesse," he added, as the big blacksmith now entered the room. Lajeunesse grinned and ducked his head. "I knew Madelinette, as did you all, when I could take her on my knee and tell her English stories, and listen to her sing French chansons—the best in the world. She has gone on; we stay where we were. But she proves her love to us, by taking her husband from Pontiac and coming back to us. May she never find a spot so good to come to and so hard to leave as Pontiac!"

He drank, and they all did the same. Draining his glass, Medallion let it fall on the stone floor. It broke into a score of pieces.

He came and shook hands with Lajeunesse. "Give her my love," he said. "Tell her the highest bidder on earth could not buy one of the kisses she gave me when she was five and I was twenty."

Then he shook hands with them all and went into the next room.

"Why did he drop his glass?" asked Gingras the shoemaker.

"That's the way of the aristocrats when it's the damnedest toast that ever was," said Duclosse the mealman. "Eh, Lajeunesse, that's so, isn't it?"

"What the devil do I know about aristocrats!" said Lajeunesse.

"You're among the best of the land, now that Madelinette's married to the Seigneur. You ought to wear a collar every day."

"Bah!" answered the blacksmith. "I'm only old Lajeunesse the blacksmith, though she's my girl, dear lads. I was Joe Lajeunesse yesterday, and I'll be Joe Lajeunesse to-morrow, and I'll die Joe Lajeunesse the forgeron—bagosh! So you take me as you find me. M'sieu' Racine doesn't marry me. And Madelinette doesn't take me to Paris and lead me round the stage and say, 'This is M'sieu' Lajeunesse, my father.' No. I'm myself, and a damn good blacksmith and nothing else am I!"

"Tut, tut, old leather-belly," said Gingras the shoemaker, whose liquor had mounted high, "you'll not need to work now. Madelinette's got double fortune. She gets thousands for a song, and she's lady of the Manor here. What's too good for you, tell me that, my forgeron?"

"Not working between meals—that's too good for me, Gingras. I'm here to earn my bread with the hands I was born with, and to eat what they earn, and live by it. Let a man live according to his gifts—bagosh! Till I'm sent for, that's what I'll do; and when time's up I'll take my hand off the bellows, and my leather apron can go to you, Gingras, for boots for a bigger fool than me."

"There's only one," said Bénoît, the ne'er-do-weel, who had been to college as a boy.

"Who's that?" said Muroc.

"You wouldn't know his name. He's trying to find eggs in last year's nest," answered Bénoît with a leer.

"He means the Seigneur," said Muroc. "Look to your son-in-law, Lajeunesse. He's kicking up a dust that'll choke Pontiac yet. It's as if there was an imp in him driving him on."

"We've had enough of the devil's dust here," said Lajeunesse. "Has he been talking to you, Muroc?"

Muroc nodded. "Treason, or thereabouts. Once, with him that's dead in the graveyard yonder, it was France we were to save and bring back the Napoleons—I have my sword yet. Now it's save Quebec. It's stand alone and have our own flag, and shout, and fight, maybe, to be free of England. Independence—that's it! One by one the English have had to go from Pontiac. Now it's M'sieu' Medallion."

"There's Shandon the Irishman gone too. M'sieu' sold him up and shipped him off," said Gingras the shoemaker.

"Tiens! the Seigneur gave him fifty dollars when he left, to help him along. He smacks and then kisses, does M'sieu' Racine."

"We've to pay tribute to the Seigneur every year, as they did in the days of Vaudreuil and Louis the Saint," said Duclosse. "I've got my notice—a bag of meal under the big tree at the Manor door."

"I've to bring a pullet and a bag of charcoal," said Muroc. "'Tis the rights of the Seigneur as of old."

"Tiens! it is my mind," said Bénoît, "that a man that nature twists in back, or leg, or body anywhere, gets a twist in's brain too. There's Parpon the dwarf—God knows, Parpon is a nut to crack!"

"But Parpon isn't married to the greatest singer in the world, though she's only the daughter of old leather-belly there," said Gingras.

"Something doesn't come of nothing, snub-nose," said Lajeunesse. "Mark you, I was born a man of fame, walking bloody paths to glory; but, by the grace of Heaven and my baptism, I became a forgeron. Let others ride to glory, I'll shoe their horses for the gallop."

"You'll be in Parliament yet, Lajeunesse," said Duclosse the mealman, who had been dozing on a pile of untired cart-wheels.

"I'll be hanged first, comrade."

"One in the family at a time," said Muroc. "There's the Seigneur. He's going into Parliament."

"He's a magistrate—that's enough," said Duclosse. "He's started the court under the big tree, as the Seigneurs did two hundred years ago. He'll want a gibbet and a gallows next."

"I should think he'd stay at home and not take more on his shoulders!" said the one-eyed shoemaker. Without a word, Lajeunesse threw a dish of water in Gingras's face. This reference to the Seigneur's deformity was unpalatable.

Gingras had not recovered from his discomfiture when all were startled by the distant blare of a bugle. They rushed to the door, and were met by Parpon the dwarf, who announced that a regiment of soldiers was marching on the village.

"'Tis what I expected after that meeting, and the Governor's visit, and the lily-flag of France on the Manor, and the body-guard and the carbines," said Muroc nervously.

"We're all in trouble again—sure," said Bénoît, and drained his glass to the last drop. "Some of us will go to gaol."

The coming of the militia had been wholly unexpected by the people of Pontiac, but the cause was not far to seek. Ever since the Governor's visit there had been sinister rumours abroad concerning

Louis Racine, which the Curé and the Avocat and others had taken pains to contradict. It was known that the Seigneur had been requested to disband his so-called company of soldiers with their ancient livery and their modern arms, and to give them up. He had disbanded the corps, but he had not given up the arms, and, for reasons unknown, the Government had not pressed the point, so far as the world knew. But it had decided to hold a district drill in this far-off portion of the Province; and this summer morning two thousand men marched upon the town and through it, horse, foot, and commissariat,[9] and Pontiac was roused out of the last-century romance the Seigneur had sought to continue, to face the actual presence of modern force and the machinery of war. Twice before had British soldiers marched into the town, the last time but a few years agone, when blood had been shed on the stones in front of the parish church. But here were large numbers of well-armed men from the Eastern parishes, English and French, with four hundred regulars to leaven the mass. Lajeunesse knew only too well what this demonstration meant.

Before the last soldier had passed through the street, he was on his way to the Seigneury.

He found Madelinette alone in the great dining-room, mending a rent in the British flag, which she was preparing for a flag-staff. When she saw him, she dropped the flag, as if startled, came quickly to him, took both his hands in hers, and kissed his cheek.

"Wonder of wonders!" she said.

"It's these soldiers," he replied shortly. "What of them?" she asked brightly.

---

[9] Civilians in uniform who function as service-providers to the army.

"Do you mean to say you don't know what their coming here means?" he asked.

"They must drill somewhere, and they are honouring Pontiac," she replied gaily, but her face flushed as she bent over the flag again.

He came and stood in front of her. "I don't know what's in your mind; I don't know what you mean to do; but I do know that M'sieu' Racine is making trouble here, and out of it you'll come more hurt than anybody."

"What has Louis done?"

"What has he done! He's been stirring up feeling against the British. What has he done!—Look at the silly customs he's got out of old coffins, to make us believe they're alive. Why did he ever try to marry you? Why did you ever marry him? You are the great singer of the world. He's a mad hunchback habitant seigneur!"

She stamped her foot indignantly, but presently she ruled herself to composure, and said quietly: "He is my husband. He is a brave man, with foolish dreams." Then with a sudden burst of tender feeling, she said: "Oh, father, father, can't you see, I loved him—that is why I married him. You ask me what I am going to do? I am going to give the rest of my life to him. I am going to stay with him, and be to him all that he may never have in this world, never—never. I am going to be to him what my mother was to you, a slave to the end—a slave who loved you, and who gave you a daughter who will do the same for her husband—"

"No matter what he does or is—eh?"

"No matter what he is."

Lajeunesse gasped. "You will give up singing! Not sing again before kings and courts, and not earn ten thousand dollars a month—more than I've earned in twenty years? You don't mean that, Madelinette."

He was hoarse with feeling, and he held out his hand pleadingly. To him it seemed that his daughter was mad; that she was throwing her life away.

"I mean that, father," she answered quietly. "There are things worth more than money."

"You don't mean to say that you can love him as he is. It isn't natural. But no, it isn't."

"What would you have said, if any one had asked you if you loved my mother that last year of her life, when she was a cripple, and we wheeled her about in a chair you made for her?"

"Don't say any more," he said slowly, and took up his hat, and kept turning it round in his hand. "But you'll prevent him getting into trouble with the Gover'ment?" he urged at last.

"I have done what I could," she answered. Then with a little gasp: "They came to arrest him a fortnight ago, but I said they should not enter the house. Havel and I prevented them—refused to let them enter. The men did not know what to do, and so they went back. And now this—!" she pointed to where the soldiers were pitching their tents in the valley below. "Since then Louis has done nothing to give trouble. He only writes and dreams. If he would but dream and no more—!" she added, half under her breath.

"We've dreamt too much in Pontiac already," said Lajeunesse, shaking his head.

Madelinette reached up her hand and laid it on his shaggy black hair. "You are a good little father, big smithy-man," she said lovingly. "You make me think of the strong men in the Niebelungen legends.[10] It must be a big horse that will take you to Walhalla with the heroes," she added.

"Such notions—there in your head," he laughed. "Try to frighten me with your big names—hein?" There was a new look in the face of father and of daughter. No mist or cloud was between them. The things they had long wished to say were uttered at last. A new faith was established between them. Since her return they had laughed and talked as of old when they had met, though her own heart was aching, and he was bitter against the Seigneur. She had kept him and the whole parish in good humour by her unconventional ways, as though people were not beginning to make pilgrimages to Pontiac to see her—people who stared at the name over the blacksmith's door, and eyed her curiously, or lay in wait about the Seigneury, that they might get a glimpse of Madame and her deformed husband. Out in the world where she was now so important, the newspapers told strange romantic tales of the great singer, wove wild and wonderful legends of her life. To her it did not matter. If she knew, she did not heed. If she heeded it—even in her heart—she showed nothing of it before the world. She knew that soon there would be wilder tales still when it was announced that she was bidding farewell to the great working world, and would live on in retirement. She had made up her mind quite how the announcement should read, and, once it was given out, nothing would induce her to change her mind. Her life was now the life of the Seigneur.

A struggle in her heart went on, but she fought it down. The lure of a great temptation from that far-off outside world was before her, but she had resolved her heart against it. In his rough but tender way

---

[10] From Norse and Germanic legend; the Niebelungen were believed to be a family of powerful warriors. Walhalla, or Valhalla, is the great hall in these legends, where the men who die in combat are taken by the Valkyries.

her father now understood, and that was a comfort to her. He felt what he could not reason upon or put into adequate words. But the confidence made him happy, and his eyes said so to her now.

"See, big smithy-man," she said gaily, "soon will be the fête of St. Jean Baptiste,[11] and we shall all be happy then. Louis has promised me to make a speech that will not be against the English, but only words which will tell how dear the old land is to us."

"Ten to one against it!" said Lajeunesse anxiously. Then he brightened as he saw a shadow cross her face. "But you can make him do anything—as you always made me," he added, shaking his tousled head and taking with a droll eagerness the glass of wine she offered him.

[11] Holiday still celebrated in Quebec (as well as several European countries) on June 24, the feast day of the Nativity of St. John the Baptist.

CHAPTER THREE

Man to Man and Steel to Steel

One evening a fortnight later Louis Racine and George Fournel, the Englishman, stood face to face in the library of the Manor House. There was antagonism and animosity in the attitude of both. Apart from the fact that Louis had succeeded to the Seigneury promised to Fournel, and sealed to him by a reputed will which had never been found, there was cause for hatred on the Englishman's part. Fournel had been an incredibly successful man. Things had come his way—wealth, and the power that wealth brings. He had but two set-backs, and the man before him in the Manor House of Pontiac was the cause of both. The last rebuff had been the succession to the Seigneury, which, curious as it might seem, had been the cherished dream of the rich man's retirement. It had been his fancy to play the Seigneur, the lord magnificent and bountiful, and he had determined to use wealth and all manner of influence to have the title of Baron of Pontiac revived—it had been obsolete for a hundred years. He leaned towards the grace of an hereditary dignity, as other retired millionaires cultivate art and letters, vainly imagining that they can wheedle civilisation and the humanities into giving them what they do not possess by nature, and fool the world at the same time.

The loss of the Seigneury had therefore cut deep, but there had been a more hateful affront still. Four years before, Louis Racine, when spasmodically practising law in Quebec, had been approached by two poor Frenchmen, who laid claim to thousands of acres of land which a Land Company, whereof George Fournel was president, was publicly exploiting for the woods and valuable minerals discovered on it. The Land Company had been composed of Englishmen only. Louis Racine, reactionary and imaginative, brilliant and free from sordidness, and openly hating the English, had taken up the case, and for two years fought it tooth and nail without pay or reward. The matter had become a *cause célèbre*, the Land Company engaging the greatest lawyers in both the English and French province. In the Supreme Court the case was lost to Louis' clients. Louis took it over to the Privy Council in London, and carried it through triumphantly and alone, proving his clients' title. His two poor Frenchmen regained their land. In payment he would accept nothing save the ordinary fees, as though it were some petty case in a county court. He had, however, made a reputation, which he had seemed not to value, save as a means of showing hostility to the governing race, and the Seigneury of Pontiac, when it fell to him, had more charms for him than any celebrity to be won at the bar. His love of the history of his country was a mania with him, and he looked forward, on arriving at Pontiac, to being the apostle of French independence on the continent. Madelinette had crossed his path in his most enthusiastic moment, when his brilliant tongue and great dreams surrounded him with a kind of glamour. He had caught her to himself out of the girl's first triumph, when her nature, tried by the strain of her first challenge to the judgment of the world, cried out for rest, for Pontiac and home, and all that was of the old life among her people.

Fournel's antipathy had only been increased by the fact that Louis Racine had married the now famous Madelinette, and his animosity extended to her.

It was not in him to understand the nature of the Frenchman, volatile, moody, chivalrous, unreasonable, the slave of ideas, the victim of sentiment. Not understanding, when he began to see that he could not attain the object of his visit, which was to secure some relics of the late Seigneur's household, he chose to be disdainful.

"You are bound to give me these things I ask for, as a matter of justice—if you know what justice means," he said at last.

"You should be aware of that," answered the Seigneur, with a kindling look. He felt every glance of Fournel's eye a contemptuous comment upon his deformity, now so egregious and humiliating. "I taught you justice once."

Fournel was not to be moved from his phlegm. He knew he could torture the man before him, and he was determined to do so, if he did not get his way upon the matter of his visit.

"You can teach me justice twice and be thanked once," he answered. "These things I ask for were much prized by my friend, the late Seigneur. I was led to expect that this Seigneury and all in it and on it should be mine. I know it was intended so. The law gives it you instead. Your technical claim has overridden my rights—you have a gift for making successful technical claims. But these old personal relics, of no monetary value—you should waive your avaricious and indelicate claim to them." He added the last words with a malicious smile, for the hardening look in Racine's face told him his request was hopeless, and he could not resist the temptation to put the matter with cutting force. Racine rose to the bait with a jump.

"Not one single thing—not one single solitary thing—!"

"The sentiment is strong if the grammar is bad," interrupted Fournel, meaning to wound wherever he found an opportunity, for the Seigneur's deformity excited in him no pity; it rather incensed him against the man, as an affront to decency and to his own just claims to the honours the Frenchman enjoyed. It was a petty resentment, but George Fournel had set his heart upon playing the grand-seigneur over the Frenchmen of Pontiac, and of ultimately leaving his fortune to the parish, if they all fell down and worshipped him and his "golden calf."

"The grammar is suitable to the case," retorted the Seigneur, his voice rising. "Everything is mine by law, and everything I will keep. If you think different, produce a will—produce a will!"

Truth was, Louis Racine would rather have parted with the Seigneury itself than with these relics asked for. They were reminiscent of the time when France and her golden-lilies brooded over his land, of the days when Louis Quatorze[12] was king. He cherished everything that had association with the days of the *old régime*, as a miner hugs his gold, or a woman her jewels. The request to give them up to this unsympathetic Englishman, who valued them because they had belonged to his friend the late Seigneur, only exasperated him.

---

[12] Louis XIV of France (1638–1715), also known as Louis the Great (*Louis le Grand*) and the Sun King, was king of France from 1643 until his death. During his long reign, France was the leading European power.

"I am ready to pay the highest possible price for them, as I have said," urged the Englishman, realising as he spoke that it was futile to urge the sale upon that basis.

"Money cannot buy the things that Frenchmen love. We are not a race of hucksters," retorted the Seigneur.

"That accounts for your envious dispositions then. You can't buy what you want—you love such curious things, I assume. So you play the dog in the manger, and won't let other decent folk buy what they want." He wilfully distorted the other's meaning, and was delighted to see the Seigneur's fingers twitch with fury. "But since you can't buy the things you love—and you seem to think you should—how do you get them? Do you come by them honestly? or do you work miracles? When a spider makes love to his lady he dances before her to infatuate her, and then in a moment of her delighted aberration snatches at her affections. Is it the way of the spider then?"

With a snarl as of a wild beast, Louis Racine sprang forward and struck Fournel in the face with his clinched fist. Then, as Fournel, blinded, staggered back upon the book-shelves, he snatched two antique swords from the wall. Throwing one on the floor in front of the Englishman, he ran to the door and locked it, and turned round, the sword grasped firmly in his hand, and white with rage.

"Spider! Spider! By Heaven, you shall have the spider dance before you!" he said hoarsely. He had mistaken Fournel's meaning. He had put the most horrible construction upon it. He thought that Fournel referred to his deformity, and had ruthlessly dragged in Madelinette as well.

He was like a being distraught. His long brown hair was tossed over his blanched forehead and piercing black eyes. His head was thrown forward even more than his deformity compelled, his white teeth showed in a grimace of hatred; he was half-crouched, like an animal ready to spring.

"Take up the sword, or I'll run you through the heart where you stand," he continued, in a hoarse whisper. "I will give you till I can count three. Then by the God in Heaven—!"

Fournel felt that he had to deal with a man demented. The blow he had received had laid open the flesh on his cheek-bone, and blood was flowing from the wound. Never in his life before had he been so humiliated. And by a Frenchman—it roused every instinct of race-hatred in him. Yet he wanted not to go at him with a sword, but with his two honest hands, and beat him into a whining submission. But the man was deformed, he had none of his own robust strength—he was not to be struck, but to be tossed out of the way like an offending child.

He staunched the blood from his face and made a step forward without a word, determined not to fight, but to take the weapon from the other's hands. "Coward!" said the Seigneur. "You dare not fight with the sword. With the sword we are even. I am as strong as you there—stronger, and I will have your blood. Coward! Coward! Coward! I will give you till I count three. *One!... Two!...*"

Fournel did not stir. He could not make up his mind what to do. Cry out? No one could come in time to prevent the onslaught—and onslaught there would be, he knew. There was a merciless hatred in the Seigneur's face, a deadly purpose in his eyes; the wild determination of a man who did not care whether he lived or died, ready to throw himself upon a hundred in his hungry rage. It seemed so mad, so monstrous, that the beautiful summer day through which came the sharp whetting of the scythe, the song of the birds, and the smell of ripening fruit and grain, should be invaded by this tragic absurdity, this human fury which must spend itself in blood.

Fournel's mind was conscious of this feeling, this sense of futile, foolish waste and disfigurement, even as the Seigneur said *'Three.'* and, rushing forward, thrust.

As Fournel saw the blade spring at him, he dropped on one knee, caught it with his left hand as it came, and wrenched it aside. The blade lacerated his fingers and his palm, but he did not let go till he had seized the sword at his feet with his right hand. Then, springing up with it, he stepped back quickly and grasped his weapon fiercely enough now.

Yet, enraged as he was, he had no wish to fight; to involve himself in a *fracas* which might end in tragedy and the courts of the land. It was a high price to pay for any satisfaction he might have in this affair. If the Seigneur were killed in the encounter—he must defend himself now—what a miserable notoriety and possible legal penalty and public punishment! For who could vouch for the truth of his story? Even if he wounded Racine only, what a wretched story to go abroad: that he had fought with a hunchback—a hunchback who knew the use of the sword, which he did not, but still a hunchback!

"Stop this nonsense," he said, as Louis Racine prepared to attack again. "Don't be a fool. The game isn't worth the candle."

"One of us does not leave this room alive," said the Seigneur. "You care for life. You love it, *and you can t buy what you love from me.* I don't care for life, and I would gladly die, to see your blood flow. Look, it's flowing down your face; it's dripping from your hand, and there shall be more dripping soon. On guard!"

He suddenly attacked with a fierce energy, forcing Fournel back upon the wall. He was not a first-class swordsman, but he had far more knowledge of the weapon than his opponent, and he had no scruple about using his knowledge. Fournel fought with desperate alertness, yet awkwardly, and he could not attack; it was all that he could do, all that he knew how to do, to defend himself. Twice again did the Seigneur's weapon draw blood, once from the shoulder and once from the leg of his opponent, and the blood was flowing from each wound. After the second injury they stood panting for a moment. Now the outside world was shut out from Fournel's senses as it was from Louis Racine's. The only world they knew was this cool room, whose oak floors were browned by the slow searching stains of Time, and darkened by the footsteps of six generations that had come and gone through the old house. The books along the walls seemed to cry out against the unseemly and unholy strife. But now both men were in that atmosphere of supreme egoism where only their two selves moved, and where the only thing that mattered on earth was the issue of this strife. Fournel could only think of how to save his life, and to do that he must become the aggressor, for his wounds were bleeding hard, and he must have more wounds, if the fight went on without harm to the Seigneur.

"You know now what it is to insult a Frenchman—*On guard!*" again cried the Seigneur, in a shriller voice, for everything in him was pitched to the highest note.

He again attacked, and the sound of the large swords meeting clashed on the soft air. As they struggled, a voice came ringing through the passages, singing a bar from an opera:

"Oh eager golden day, Oh happy evening hour,

Behold my lover cometh from fields of wrath and hate!
Sheathed is his sword; he cometh to my bower;
In war he findeth honour, and love within the gate."

The voice came nearer and nearer. It pierced the tragic separateness of the scene of blood. It reached the ears of the Seigneur, and a look of pain shot across his face. Fournel was only dimly aware of the voice, for he was hard pressed, and it seemed to come from infinite distances. Presently the voice stopped, and someone tried the door of the room.

It was Madelinette. Astonished at finding it locked, she stood still a moment uncertain what to do. Then the sounds of the struggle within came to her ears. She shook the door, leaned her shoulders against it, and called, "Louis! Louis!" Suddenly she darted away, found Havel the faithful servant in the passage, and brought him swiftly to the door. The man sprang upon it, striking with his shoulder. The lock gave, the door flew open, and Madelinette stepped swiftly into the room, in time to see George Fournel sway and fall, his sword rattling on the hard oak floor.

"Oh, what have you done, Louis!" she cried, then added hurriedly to Havel: "Draw the blind there, shut the door, and tell Madame Marie to bring some water quickly."

The silent servant vanished, and she dropped on her knees beside the bleeding and insensible man, and lifted his head.

"He insulted you and me, and I've killed him, Madelinette," said Louis hoarsely.

A horrified look came to her face, and she hurriedly and tremblingly opened Fournel's waistcoat and shirt, and felt his heart.

She was freshly startled by a struggle behind her, and, turning quickly, she saw Madame Marie holding the Seigneur's arm to prevent him from ending his own life.

She sprang up and laid her hand upon her husband's arm. "He is not dead—you need not do it, Louis," she said quietly. There was no alarm, no undue excitement in her face now. She was acting with good presence of mind. A new sense was working in her. Something had gone from her suddenly where her husband was concerned, and something else had taken its place. An infinite pity, a bitter sorrow, and a gentle command were in her eyes all at once-new vistas of life opened before her, all in an instant.

"He is not dead, and there is no need to kill yourself, Louis," she repeated, and her voice had a command in it that was not to be gainsaid. "Since you have vindicated your honour, you will now help me to set this business right."

Madame Marie was on her knees beside the insensible man. "No, he is not dead, thank God!" she murmured, and while Havel stripped the arm and leg, she poured some water between Fournel's lips. Her long experience as the Little Chemist's wife served her well now.

Now that the excitement was over, Louis collapsed. He swayed and would have fallen, but Madelinette caught him, helped him to the sofa, and, forcing him gently down on his side, adjusted a pillow for him, and turned to the wounded man again.

An hour went busily by in the closely-curtained room, and at last George Fournel, conscious, and with wounds well bandaged, sat in a big arm-chair, glowering round him. At his first coming—to, Louis Racine, at his wife's insistence, had come and offered his hand, and made apology for assaulting him in his own house.

Fournel's reply had been that he wanted to hear no more fool's talk and to have no more fool's doings, and that one day he hoped to take his pay for the day's business in a satisfactory way.

Madelinette made no apology, said nothing, save that she hoped he would remain for a few days till he was recovered enough to be moved. He replied that he would leave as soon as his horses were ready, and refused to take food or drink from their hands. His servant was brought from the Louis Quinze Hotel, and through him he got what was needed for refreshment, and requested that no one of the household should come near him. At night, in the darkness, he took his departure, no servant of the household in attendance. But as he got into the carriage, Madelinette came quickly to him, and said:

"I would give ten years of my life to undo to-day's work."

"I have no quarrel with you, Madame," he said gloomily, raised his hat, and was driven away.

CHAPTER FOUR

Madelinette Makes a Discovery

The national fête of the summer was over. The day had been successful, more successful indeed than any within the memory of the inhabitants; for the English and French soldiers joined in the festivities without any intrusion of racial spirit, but in the very essence and soul of good-fellowship. The General had called at the Manor, and paid his respects to the Seigneur, who received him abstractedly if not coolly, but Madelinette had captured his imagination and his sympathies. He was fond of music for an Englishman, and with a ravishing charm she sang for him a bergerette[13] of the eighteenth century and then a ballad of Shakespeare's set to her own music. She was so anxious that the great holiday should pass off without one untoward incident, that she would have resorted to any fair device to attain the desired end. The General could help her by his influence and instructions, and if the soldiers—regulars and militia—joined in the celebrations

---

[13] A traditional rustic French song, also known as a Shepherdess' air.

harmoniously, and with goodwill, a long step would be made towards undoing the harm that Louis had done, and maybe influencing him towards a saner, wiser view of things. He had changed much since the fateful day when he had forced George Fournel to fight him; had grown more silent, and had turned grey. His eyes had become by turns watchful and suspicious, gloomy and abstracted; and his speech knew the same variations; now bitter and cynical, now sad and distant, and all the time his eyes seemed to grow darker and his face paler. But however moody and variable and irascible he might be with others, however unappeasable, with Madelinette he struggled to be gentle, and his petulance gave way under the intangible persuasiveness of her words and will, which had the effect of command. Under this influence he had prepared the words which he was to deliver at the Fête. They were full of veneration for past traditions, but were not at variance with a proper loyalty to the flag under which they lived, and if the English soldiery met the speech with genial appreciation the day might end in a blessing—and surely blessings were overdue in Madelinette's life in Pontiac.

It had been as she worked for and desired, thanks to herself and the English General's sympathetic help. Perhaps his love of music made him better understand what she wanted, made him even forgiving of the Seigneur's strained manner; but certain it is that the day, begun with uneasiness on the part of the people of Pontiac, who felt themselves under surveillance, ended in great good-feeling and harmless revelry; and it was also certain that the Seigneur's speech gained him an applause that surprised him and momentarily appeased his vanity. The General gave him a guard of honour of the French Militia in keeping with his position as Seigneur; and this, with Madelinette's presence at his elbow, restrained him in his speech when he would have broken from the limits of propriety in the intoxication of his eager eloquence. But he spoke with moderation, standing under the British Flag on the platform, and at the last he said:

"A flag not our own floats over us now; guarantees us against the malice of the world and assures us in our laws and religion; but there is another flag which in our tearful memories is as dear to us now as it was at Carillon and Lévis.[14] It is the flag of memory—of language and of race, the emblem of our past upon our hearthstones; and the great country that rules us does not deny us reverence to it. Seeing it, we see the history of our race from Charlemagne[15] to this day, and we have a pride in that history which England does not rebuke, a pride which is just and right. It is fitting that we should have a day of commemoration. Far off in France burns the light our fathers saw and were glad. And we in Pontiac have a link that binds us to the old home. We have ever given her proud remembrance—we now give her art and song."

With these words, and turning to his wife, he ended, and cries of "Madame Madelinette! Madame Madelinette!" were heard everywhere. Even the English soldiers cheered, and Madelinette sang à la Claire Fontaine, three verses in French and one in English, and the whole valley rang with the refrain sung at the topmost pitch by five thousand voices:

[14] François de Gaston, Chevalier de Lévis (1719–1787) was second in command to Louis-Joseph de Montcalm in the defence of New France during the Seven Years' War. In the Battle of Carillon, Lévis was a key figure in the successful defeat of a much larger British frontal assault on the Fort of Carillon.

[15] Charlemagne (c. 748–814 CE), also known as Charles the Great, united much of Western Europe into the Carolingian Empire. The French monarchy claimed descent from Charlemagne's empire (as did the German monarchy).

"I'ya longtemps que je t'aime,

Jamais je ne t'oublierai."

The day of pleasure done and dusk settled on Pontiac and on the encampment of soldiers in the valley, a light still burned in the library at the Manor House long after midnight. Madelinette had gone to bed, but, excited by the events of the day, she could not sleep, and she went down to the library to read. But her mind wandered still, and she sat mechanically looking before her at a picture of the father of the late Seigneur, which was let into the moulding of the oak wall. As she looked abstractedly and yet with the intensity of the preoccupied mind, her eye became aware of a little piece of wood let into the moulding of the frame. The light of the hanging lamp was full on it.

This irregularity began to perplex her eye. Presently it intruded on her reverie. Still busy with her thoughts, she knelt upon the table beneath the picture and pressed the irregular piece of wood. A spring gave, the picture came slowly away from the frame, and disclosed a small cupboard behind. In this cupboard were a few books, an old silver-handled pistol, and a packet. Madelinette's reverie was broken now. She was face to face with discovery and mystery. Her heart stood still with fear. After an instant of suspense, she took out the packet and held it to the light. She gave a smothered cry.

It was the will of the late Seigneur.

CHAPTER FIVE

What Will She Do With It?

Madelinette's heart stood still. Louis was no longer—indeed, never had been—Seigneur of Pontiac, and they had no right there, had never had any right there. They must leave this place which was to Louis the fetish of his soul, the small compensation fate had made him for the trouble nature had cynically laid upon him. He had clung to it as a drowning man clings to a spar. To him it was the charter from which he could appeal to the world as the husband of Madelinette Lajeunesse. To him it was the name, the dignity, and the fortune he brought her. It was the one thing that saved him from a dire humiliation; it was the vantage-ground from which he appealed to her respect, the flaming testimony of his own self-esteem. Every hour since his trouble had come upon him, since Madelinette's great fame had come to her, he had protested to himself that it was honour for honour; and every day he had laboured, sometimes how fantastically, how futilely! to dignify his position, to enhance his importance in her eyes. She had understood it all, had read him to the last letter in the alphabet of his mind and heart. She had realised the consternation of the people, and she knew that, for her sake, and because the Curé had commanded, all the obsolete claims he had made were responded to by the people. Certainly he had affected them by his eloquence and his fiery kindness, but at the same time they had shrewdly smelt the treason underneath his ardour. There was a definite limit to their loyalty to him; and, deprived of the Seigneury, he would count for nothing.

A hundred thoughts like these went through her mind as she stood by the table under the hanging lamp, her face white as the loose robe she wore, her eyes hot and staring, her figure rigid as stone.

To-morrow—how could she face to-morrow, and Louis! How could she tell him this! How could she say to him, "Louis, you are no longer Seigneur. The man you hate, he who is your inveterate enemy, who has every reason to exact from you the last tribute of humiliation, is Seigneur here!" How could she face the despair of the man whose life was one inward fever, one long illusion, which was yet only half an illusion, since he was forever tortured by suspicion; whose body was wearing itself out, and spirit was destroying itself in the struggle of a vexed imagination!

She knew that Louis' years were numbered. She knew that this blow would break him body and soul. He could never survive the humiliation. His sensitiveness was a disease, his pride was the only thing that kept him going; his love of her, strong as it was, would be drowned in an imagined shame!

It was midnight. She was alone with this secret. She held the paper in her hand, which was at once Louis' sentence or his charter of liberty. A candle was at her hand, the doors were shut, the blinds drawn, the house a frozen silence—how cold she was, though it was the deep of summer! She shivered from head to foot, and yet all day the harvest sun had drenched the room in its heat.

Yet her blood might run warm again, her cold cheeks might regain their colour, her heart beat quietly, if this paper were no more! The thought made her shrink away from herself, as it were, yet she caught up the candle and lighted it.

For Louis. For Louis, though she would rather have died than do it for herself. To save to Louis what was, to his imagination, the one claim he had upon her respect and the world's. After all, how little was it in value or in dignity! How little she cared for it! One year of her voice could earn two such Seigneuries as this. And the honour—save that it was Pontiac—it was naught to her. In all her life she had never done or said a dishonourable thing. She had never lied, she had never deceived, she had never done aught that might not have been written down and published to all the world. Yet here, all at once, she was faced with a vast temptation, to do a deed, the penalty of which was an indelible shame.

What injury would it do to George Fournel! He was used now to his disappointment; he was rich; he had no claims upon Pontiac; there was no one but himself to whom it mattered, this little Seigneury. What he did not know did not exist, so far as himself was concerned. How easily could it all be made right some day! She felt as though she were suffocating, and she opened the window a little very softly. Then she lit the candle tremblingly, watched the flame gather strength, and opened out the will. As she did so, however, the smell of a clover field, which is as honey, came stealing through the room, and all at once a strange association of ideas flashed into her brain.

She recalled one summer day long ago, when, in the church of St. Saviour's, the smell of the clover fields came through the open doors and windows, and her mind had kept repeating mechanically, till she fell asleep, the text of the Curé's sermon—"As ye sow, so also shall ye reap."

That placid hour which had no problems, no cares, no fears, no penalties in view, which was filled with the richness of a blessed harvest and the plenitude of innocent youth, came back on her now in the moment of her fierce temptation.

She folded up the paper slowly, a sob came in her throat, she blew out the candle, and put the will back in the cupboard. The faint click of the spring as she closed the panel seemed terribly loud to her. She started and looked timorously round. The blood came back to her face—she flushed crimson with guilt. Then she turned out the lighted lamp and crept away up the stairs to her room.

She paused beside Louis' bed. He was moving restlessly in his sleep; he was murmuring her name. With a breaking sigh she crept into bed slowly and lay like one who had been beaten, bruised, and shamed.

At last, before the dawn, she fell asleep. She dreamed that she was in prison and that George Fournel was her jailor.

She waked to find Louis at her bedside.

"I am holding my seigneurial court to-day," he said.

CHAPTER SIX

The One Who Saw

All day and every day Madelinette's mind kept fastening itself upon one theme, kept turning to one spot. In her dreams she saw the hanging lamp, the moving panel, the little cupboard, the fatal paper. Waking and restlessly busy, she sometimes forgot it for a moment, but remembrance would come back with painful force, and her will must govern her hurt spirit into quiet resolution. She had such a sense of humiliation as though some one dear to her had committed a crime against herself. Two persons were in her— Madelinette Lajeunesse, the daughter of the village blacksmith, brought up in the peaceful discipline of her religion, shunning falsehood and dishonour with a simple proud self-respect; and Madame Racine, the great singer, who had touched at last the heart of things; and, with the knowledge, had thrown aside past principles and convictions to save her stricken husband from misery and humiliation—to save his health, his mind, his life maybe.

The struggle of conscience and expediency, of principle and womanliness wore upon her, taking away the colour from her cheeks, but spiritualising her face, giving the large black eyes an expression of rare intensity, so that the Avocat in his admiration called her Madonna, and the Curé came oftener to the Manor House with a fear in his heart that all was not well. Yet he was met by her cheerful smile, by her quiet sense of humour, by the touching yet not demonstrative devotion of the wife to the husband, and a varying and impulsive adoration of the wife by the husband. One day when the Curé was with the Seigneur, Madelinette entered upon them. Her face was pale though composed, yet her eyes had a look of abstraction or detachment. The Curé's face brightened at her approach. She wore a simple white gown with a bunch of roses at the belt, and a broad hat lined with red that shaded her face and gave it a warmth it did not possess.

"Dear Madame!" said the Curé, rising to his feet and coming towards her.

"I have told you before that I will have nothing but 'Madelinette,' dear Curé," she replied, with a smile, and gave him her hand. She turned to Louis, who had risen also, and putting a hand on his arm pressed him gently into his chair, then, with a swift, almost casual, caress of his hair, placed on the table the basket of flowers she was carrying, and began to arrange them.

"Dear Louis," she said presently, and as though *en passant*, "I have dismissed Tardif to-day—I hope you won't mind these dull domestic details, Curé," she added.

The Curé nodded and turned his head towards the window musingly. He was thinking that she had done a wise thing in dismissing Tardif, for the man had evil qualities, and he was hoping that he would leave the parish now.

The Seigneur nodded. "Then he will go. I have dismissed him—I have a temper—many times, but he never went. It is foolish to dismiss a man in a temper. He thinks you do not mean it. But our Madelinette there"—he turned towards the Curé now—"she is never in a temper, and every-one always knows she means what she says; and she says it as even as a clock." Then the egoist in him added: "I have power and imagination and the faculty for great things; but Madelinette has serene judgment—a tribute to you, Curé, who taught her in the old days."

"In any case, Tardif is going," she repeated quietly.

"What did he do?" said the Seigneur. "What was your grievance, beautiful Madame?"

He was looking at her with unfeigned admiration—with just such a look as was in his face the first day they met in the Avocat's house on his arrival in Pontiac. She turned and saw it, and remembered. The scene flashed before her mind. The thought of herself then, with the flush of a sunrise love suddenly rising in her heart, roused a torrent of feeling now, and it required every bit of strength she had to prevent her bursting into a passion of tears. In imagination she saw him there, a straight, slim, handsome figure, with the very vanity of proud health upon him, and ambition and passionate purpose in every line of his figure, every glance of his eyes. Now— there he was, bent, frail, and thin, with restless eyes and deep discontent in voice and manner; the curved shoulder and the head grown suddenly old; the only thing, speaking of the past, the graceful hand, filled with the illusory courage of a declining vitality. But for the nervous force in him, the latent vitality which renewed with stubborn persistence the failing forces, he was dead. The brain kept commanding the body back to life and manhood daily.

"What did Tardif do?" the Seigneur again questioned, holding out a hand to her.

She did not dare to take his hand lest her feelings should overcome her; so with an assumed gaiety she put in it a rose from her basket and said:

"He has been pilfering. Also he was insolent. I suppose he could not help remembering that I lived at the smithy once—the dear smithy," she added softly.

"I will go at once and pay the scoundrel his wages," said the Seigneur, rising, and with a nod to the Curé and his wife opened the door.

"Do not see him yourself, Louis," said Madelinette.

"Not I. Havel shall pay him and he shall take himself off to-morrow morning."

The door closed, and Madelinette was left alone with the Curé. She came to him and said with a quivering in her voice:

"He mocked Louis."

"It is well that he should go. He is a bad man and a bad servant. I know him too well."

"You see, he keeps saying"—she spoke very slowly—"that he witnessed a will the Seigneur made in favour of Monsieur Fournel. He thinks us interlopers, I suppose."

The Curé put a hand on hers gently. "There was a time when I felt that Monsieur Fournel was the legal heir to the Seigneury, for Monsieur de la Rivière had told me there was such a will; but since then I have changed my mind. Your husband is the natural heir, and it is only just that the Seigneury should go on in the direct line. It is best."

"Even with all Louis' mistakes?"

"Even with them. You have set them right, and you will keep him within the bounds of wisdom and prudence. You are his guardian angel, Madelinette."

She looked up at him with a pensive smile and a glance of gratitude.

"But suppose that will—if there is one—exists, see how false our position!"

"Do you think it is mere accident that the will has never been found—if it was not destroyed by the Seigneur himself before he died? No, there is purpose behind it, with which neither you or I or Louis have anything to do. Ah, it is good to have you here in this Seigneury, my child! What you give us will return to you a thousandfold. Do not regret the world and your work there. You will go back all too soon."

She was about to reply when the Seigneur again entered the room.

"I made up my mind that he should go at once, and so I've sent him word—the rat!"

"I will leave you two to be drowned in the depths of your own intelligence," said Madelinette; and taking her empty basket left the room.

A strange compelling feeling drove her to the library where the fateful panel was. With a strange sense that her wrong-doing was modified by the fact, she had left the will where she had found it. She had a superstition that fate would deal less harshly with her if she did. It was not her way to temporise. She had concealed the discovery of the will with an unswerving determination. It was for Louis, it was for his peace, for the ease of his fading life, and she had no repentance. Yet there it was, that curious, useless concession to old prejudices, the little touch of hypocrisy—she left the will where she had found it. She had never looked at it since, no matter how great the temptation, and sometimes this was overpowering.

To-day it overpowered her. The house was very still and the blinds were drawn to shut out the heat, but the soft din of the locusts came through the windows. Her household were all engaged elsewhere. She shut the doors of the little room, and kneeling on the table touched the spring. The panel came back and disclosed the cupboard. There lay the will. She took it up and opened it. Her eyes went dim on the instant, and she leaned her forehead against the wall sick at heart.

As she did so a sudden gust of wind drove in the blind of the window. She started, but saw what it was, and hastily putting the will back, closed the panel, and with a fast-beating heart, left the room.

Late that evening she found a letter on her table addressed to herself. It ran:

"You've shipped me off like dirt. You'll be shipped off, Madame, double quick. I've got what'll bring the right owner here. You'll soon hear from

"TARDIF."

In terror she hastened to the library and sprung the panel. The will was gone.

Tardif was on his way with it to George Fournel.

CHAPTER SEVEN

The Pursuit

There was but one thing to do. She must go straight to George Fournel at Quebec. She knew only too well that Tardif was speeding thither as fast as horses could carry him. He had had several hours' start, but there was still a chance of overtaking him. And suppose she overtook him? She could not decide definitely what she should do, but she would do anything, sacrifice anything, to secure again that fatal document which, in George Fournel's hands, must bring a collapse worse than death. A dozen plans flashed before her, and now that her mind was set upon the thing, compunction would not stay her. She had gone so far, she was prepared to go further to save this Seigneury to Louis. She put in her pocket the silver-handled pistol from the fatal cupboard.

In an hour from the time she found the note, the horses and coach were at the door, and the faithful Havel, cloaked and armed, was ready for the journey. A note to Louis, with the excuse of a sudden and important call to Quebec, which he was to construe into business concerning her profession; hurried yet careful arrangements for his comfort during her absence; a letter to the

Curé begging of him a daily visit to the Manor House; and then, with the flurried Madame Marie, she entered the coach with Havel on the box, and they were off.

The coach rattled through the village and stopped for a moment at the smithy. A few words of cheerful good-bye to her father—she carried the spring in her face and the summer of gaiety in her face however sore her heart was—and they were once more upon the road.

Their first stage was twenty-five miles, and it led through the ravine where Parpon and his comrades had once sought to frighten George Fournel. As they passed the place Madelinette shuddered, and she remembered Fournel's cynical face as he left the house three months ago. She felt that it would not easily soften to mercy or look upon her trouble with a human eye, if once the will were in his hands. It was a silent journey, but Madame Marie asked no questions, and there was comfort in her unspoken sympathy.

Five hours, and at midnight they arrived at the end of the first stage of their journey, at the village tavern of St. Stanislaus. Here Madame Marie urged Madelinette to stay and sleep, but this she refused to do, if horses could be got to go forward. The sight of two gold pieces made the thing possible in the landlord's eyes, and Madame Marie urged no more, but found some refreshment, of which she gently insisted that Madelinette should partake. In another hour from their arrival they were on the road again, with the knowledge that Tardif had changed horses and gone forward four hours before, boasting as he went that when the bombshell he was carrying should burst, the country would stay awake o' nights for a year.

Madelinette herself had made the inquiries of the landlord, whose easily-bought obsequiousness now knew no bounds, and he gave a letter to Havel to hand to his cousin the landlord at the next change, which, he said, would be sure to secure them the best of accommodation and good horses.

As the night grew to morning, Madelinette drooped a little, and Madame Marie, who had, to her own anger and disgust, slept three hours or more, quietly drew Madelinette towards her. With a little sob the girl—for what was she but a girl—let her head drop on the old woman's shoulder, and she fell into a troubled sleep, which lasted till, in the flush of sunrise, they drew up at the solitary inn on the outskirts of the village of Beaugard. They had come fifty miles since the evening before.

Here Madelinette took Havel into her confidence, in so far as to tell him that Tardif had stolen a valuable paper from her, the loss of which might bring most serious consequences.

Whatever Havel had suspected he was the last man in the world to show or tell. But before leaving the Manor House of Pontiac he had armed himself with pistols, in the grim hope that he might be required to use them. Havel had been used hard in the world, Madelinette had been kind to him, and he was ready to show his gratitude—and he little recked[16] what form it might take. When he found that they were following Tardif, and for what purpose, an ugly joy filled his heart, and he determined on revenge—so long delayed—on the scoundrel who had once tried to turn the parish against him by evil means. He saw that his pistols were duly primed, he learned that Tardif had passed but two hours before, boasting again that Europe would have gossip for a year, once he reached

---

[16] Took heed; felt concern about.

Quebec. Tardif too had paid liberally for his refreshment and his horses, for here he had taken a carriage, and had swaggered like a trooper in a conquered country.

Havel had every hope of overtaking Tardif, and so he told Madelinette, adding that he would secure the paper for her at any cost. She did not quite know what Havel meant, but she read purpose in his eye, and when Havel said: "I won't say 'Stop thief' many times," she turned away without speaking—she was choked with anxiety. Yet in her own pocket was a little silver-handled pistol.

It was true that Tardif was a thief, but she knew that his theft would be counted a virtue before the world. This she could not tell Havel, but when the critical moment came—if it did come—she would then act upon the moment's inspiration. If Tardif was a thief, what was she!—But this she could not tell Havel or the world. Even as she thought it for this thousandth time, her face flushed deeply, and a mist came before her eyes. But she hardened her heart and gave orders to proceed as soon as the horses were ready. After a hasty breakfast they were again on their way, and reached the third stage of their journey by eleven o'clock. Tardif had passed two hours before.

So, for two days they travelled, with no sleep save what they could catch as the coach rolled on. They were delayed three hours at one inn because of the trouble in getting horses, since it appeared that Tardif had taken the only available pair in the place; but a few gold pieces brought another pair galloping from a farm two miles away, and they were again on the road. Fifty miles to go, and Tardif with three hours' start of them! Unless he had an accident there was faint chance of overtaking him, for at this stage he had taken to the saddle again. As time had gone on, and the distance between them and Quebec had decreased, Madelinette had grown paler and stiller. Yet she was considerate of Madame Marie, and more than once insisted on Havel lying down for a couple of hours, and herself made him a strengthening bowl of soup at the kitchen fire of the inn. Meanwhile she inquired whether it might be possible to get four horses at the next change, and she offered five gold pieces to a man who would ride on ahead of them and secure the team.

Some magic seemed to bring her the accomplishment of the impossible, for even as she made the offer, and the downcast looks of the landlord were assuring her that her request was futile, there was the rattle of hoofs without, and a petty Government official rode up. He had come a journey of three miles only, and his horse was fresh. Agitated, yet ruling herself to composure, Madelinette approached him and made her proposal to him. He was suspicious, as became a petty Government official, and replied sullenly. She offered him money—before the landlord, unhappily—and his refusal was now unnecessarily bitter. She turned away sadly, but Madame Marie had been roused by the official's churlishness, and for once the placid little body spoke in that vulgar tongue which needs no interpretation. She asked the fellow if he knew to whom he had been impolite, to whom he had refused a kindly act.

"You—you, a *habitant* road-watcher, a pound-keeper, a village tax-collector, or something less!" she said. "You to refuse the great singer Madelinette Lajeunesse, the wife of the Seigneur of Pontiac, the greatest patriot in the land; to refuse her whom princes are glad to serve—" She stopped and gasped her indignation.

A hundred speeches and a hundred pounds could not have done so much. The *habitant* official stared in blank amazement, the landlord took a glass of brandy to steady himself.

"The Lajeunesse—the Lajeunesse, the singer of all the world—ah, why did she not say so then!" said the churl. "What would I not do for her! Money—no, it is nothing, but the Lajeunesse, I myself would give my horse to hear her sing."

"Tell her she can have M'sieu's horse," said the landlord, excitedly interposing.

"Tiens, who the devil—the horse is mine! If Madame—if she will but let me offer it to her myself!" said the agitated official. "I sing myself—I know what singing is. I have sung in an opera—a sentinel in armour I was. Ah, but bring me to her, and you shall see what I will do, by grace of heaven! I will marry you if you haven't a husband," he added with ardour to the dumfounded Madame Marie, who hurried to the adjoining room.

An instant afterwards the official was making an oration in tangled sentences which brought him a grateful smile and a hand-clasp from Madelinette. She could not prevent him from kissing her hand, she could not refrain from laughing when, outside the room, he tried to kiss Madame Marie. She was astounded, however, an hour later, to see him still at the inn door, marching up and down, a whip in his hand. She looked at him reproachfully, indignantly.

"Why are you not on the way?" she asked.

"Your man, that M'sieu' Havel, has rode on; I am to drive," he said. "Yes, Madame, it is my everlasting honour that I am to drive you. Havel has a good horse, the horse has a good rider, you have a good servant in me. I, Madame, have a good mistress in you—I am content. I am overjoyed—I am proud—I am ready, I, Pierre Lapierre."

The churlish official had gone back to the natural state of an excitable *habitant*, ready to give away his heart or lose his head at an instant's notice, the temptation being sufficient. Madelinette was frightened. She knew well why Havel had ridden on ahead without her permission, and shaking hands with the landlord and getting into the coach, she said hastily to her new coachman: "Lose not an instant. Drive hard."

They reached the next change by noon, and here they found four horses awaiting them. Tardif, and Havel also, had come and gone. An hour's rest, and they were away again upon the last stage of the journey. They should reach Quebec soon after dusk, all being well. At first, Lapierre the official had been inclined to babble, but at last he relieved his mind by interjections only. He kept shaking his head wisely, as though debating on great problems, and he drove his horses with a master-hand—he had once been a coach driver on that long river-road, which in summer makes a narrow ribbon of white, mile for mile with the St. Lawrence from east to west. This was the proudest moment of his life. He knew great things were at stake, and they had to do with the famous singer, Lajeunesse; and what tales for his grandchildren in years to come!

The flushed and comfortable Madame Marie sat upright in the coach, holding the hand of her mistress, and Madelinette grew paler as the miles diminished between her and Quebec. Yet she was quiet and unmoving, now and then saying an encouraging word to Lapierre, who smacked his lips for miles afterwards, and took out of his horses their strength and paces by masterly degrees. So that when, at last, on the hill they saw far off the spires of Quebec, the team was swinging as steadily on as though they had not come twenty-five miles already. This was a moment of pride for Lapierre, but of apprehension for Madelinette. At the last two inns on the road she had got news of both Tardif and Havel. Tardif had had the final start of half-an-hour. A half-hour's start, and fifteen miles to go! But one thing was sure, Havel, the wiry Havel, was the better man, with sounder nerve and a fostered strength.

Yet, as they descended the hill and plunged into the wild wooded valley, untenanted and uncivilised, where the road wound and curved among giant boulders and twisted through ravines and gorges, her heart fell within her. Evening was at hand, and in the thick forest the shadows were heavy, and night was settling upon them before its time.

They had not gone a mile, however, when, as they swung creaking round a great boulder, Lapierre pulled up his horses with a loud exclamation, for almost under his horses' feet lay a man apparently dead, his horse dead beside him.

It was Havel. In an instant Madelinette and Madame Marie were bending over him. The widow of the Little Chemist had skill and presence of mind.

"He is not dead, dear mine," said she in a low voice, feeling Havel's heart.

"Thank God," was all that Madelinette could say. "Let us lift him into the coach."

Now Lapierre was standing beside them, the reins in his hand. "Leave that to me," he said, and passed the reins into Madame Marie's hands, then with muttered imprecations on persons unmentioned he lifted up the slight form of Havel, and carried him to the coach. Meanwhile Madelinette had stooped to a little stream at the side of the road, and filled her silver drinking-cup with water.

As she bent over Havel and sprinkled his face, Lapierre examined the insensible man.

"He is but stunned," he said. "He will come to in a moment."

Then he went to the spot where Havel had lain, and found a pistol lying at the side of the road. Examining it, he found it had been discharged-both barrels. Rustling with importance he brought it to Madelinette, nodding and looking wise, yet half timorous too in sharing in so remarkable a business. Madelinette glanced at the pistol, her lips tightened, and she shuddered. Havel had evidently failed, and she must face the worst. Yet now that it had come, she was none the less determined to fight on.

Havel opened his eyes and looked round in a startled way. He saw Madelinette.

"Ah, Madame, Madame, pardon! He got away. I fired twice and winged him, but he shot my horse and I fell on my head. He has got away. What time is it, Madame?" he suddenly asked. She told him. "Ah, it is too late," he added. "It happened over half-an-hour ago. Unless he is badly hurt and has fallen by the way, he is now in the city. Madame, I have failed you—pardon, Madame!"

She helped him to sit up, and made a cushion of her cloak for his head, in a corner of the coach. "There is nothing to ask pardon for, Havel," she said; "you did your best. It was to be—that's all. Drink the brandy now."

A moment afterwards Lapierre was on the box, Madame Marie was inside, and Madelinette said to the coachman:

"Drive hard—the White Calvary by the church of St. Mary Magdalene."

In another hour the coach drew up by the White Calvary, where a soft light burned in memory of some departed soul.

The three alighted. Madelinette whispered to Havel, he got up on the box beside Lapierre, and the coach rattled away to a tavern, as the two women disappeared swiftly into the darkness.

CHAPTER EIGHT

Face to Face

As the two approached the mansion where George Fournel lived, they saw the door open and a man come hurriedly out into the street. He wore his wrist in a sling.

Madelinette caught Madame Marie's arm. She did not speak, but her heart sank within her. The man was Tardif.

He saw them and shuffled over.

"Ha, Madame," he said, "he has the will, and I've not done with you yet—you'll see." Then, shaking a fist in Madelinette's face, he clattered off into the darkness.

They crossed the street, and Madame Marie knocked at Fournel's door. It was at once opened, and Madelinette announced herself. The servant stared stonily at first, then, as she mentioned her name and he saw her face, he suddenly became servile, and asked them into a small waiting-room. Monsieur Fournel was at home, and should be informed at once of Madame's arrival.

A few moments later the servant, somewhat graver, but as courteous still, came to say that Monsieur would receive her in his library. Madelinette turned towards Madame Marie. The servant understood.

"I shall see that the lady has refreshment," he said. "Will Madame perhaps care for refreshment—and a mirror, before Monsieur has the honour?—Madame has travelled far."

In spite of the anxiety of the moment and the great matters at stake, Madelinette could not but smile. "Thank you," she said, "I hope I'm not so unpresentable."

"A little dust here and there perhaps, Madame," he said, with humble courtesy.

Madelinette was not so heroical as to undervalue the suggestion. Lives perhaps were in the balance, but she was a woman, and who could tell what slight influences might turn the scale!

The servant saw her hesitation. "If Madame will but remain here, I will bring what is necessary," he said, and was gone. In a moment he appeared again with a silver basin, a mirror, and a few necessaries of the toilet.

"I suppose, Madame," said the servant, with fluttered anxiety, to show that he knew who she was, "I suppose you have had sometimes to make rough shifts, even in palaces."

She gave him a gold piece. It cheered her in the moment to think that in this forbidding house, on a forbidding mission, to a forbidding man, she had one friend. She made a hasty toilet, and but for the great paleness of her cheeks, no traces remained of the three days' travel with their hardship and anxiety. Presently, as the servant ushered her into the presence of George Fournel, even the paleness was warmed a little by the excitement of the moment.

Fournel was standing with his back to the door, looking out into the moonlit night. As she entered he quickly drew the curtains of the windows and turned towards his visitor, a curious, hard, disdainful look in his face. In his hands he held a paper which she knew only too well.

"Madame," he said, and bowed. Then he motioned her to a chair. He took one himself and sat down beside the great oak writing-desk and waited for her to speak—waited with a look which sent the blood from her heart to colour her cheeks and forehead.

She did not speak, however, but looked at him fearlessly. It was impossible for her to humble herself before the latent insolence of his look. It seemed to degrade her out of all consideration. He felt the courage of her defiance, and it moved him. Yet he could but speak in cynical suggestion.

"You had a long, hard, and adventurous journey," he said. He rose suddenly and drew a tray towards him. "Will you not have some refreshment?" he added, in an even voice. "I fear you have not had time to seek it at an inn. Your messenger has but just gone."

It was impossible for him to do justice to himself, or to let his hospitality rest upon its basis of natural courtesy. It was clear that he was moved with accumulated malice, and he could not hide it.

"Your servant has been hospitable," she said, her voice trembling a little. She plunged at once into the business of her visit.

"Monsieur, that paper you hold—" she stopped for an instant, able to go no further.

"Ah, this—this document you have sent me," he said, opening it with an assumed carelessness. "Your servant had an accident—I suppose we may call it that privately—as he came. He was fired at— was wounded. You will share with me the hope that the highwayman who stopped him may be brought to justice, though, indeed, your man Tardif left him behind in the dust. Perhaps you came upon him, Madame—hein?"

She steeled herself. Too much was at stake; she could not resent his hateful implications now.

"Tardif was not my messenger, Monsieur, as you know. Tardif was the thief of that document in your hands."

"Yes, this—will!" he said musingly, an evil glitter in his eyes. "Its delivery has been long delayed. Posts and messengers are slow from Pontiac."

"Monsieur will hear what I have to say? You have the will, your rights are in your hands. Is not that enough?"

"It is not enough," he answered, in a grating voice. "Let us be plain then, Madame, and as simple as you please. You concealed this will. Not Tardif but yourself is open to the law."

She shrank under the brutality of his manner, but she ruled herself to outward composure. She was about to reply when he added, with a sneer: "Avarice is a debasing vice—Thou shalt not covet thy neighbour's house! Thou shalt not steal!"

"Monsieur," she said calmly, "it would have been easy to destroy the will. Have you not thought of that?"

For a moment he was taken aback, but he said harshly: "If crime were always intelligent, it would have fewer penalties."

She shrank again under the roughness of his words. But she was fighting for an end that was dear to her soul, and she answered:

"It was not lack of intelligence, but a sense of honour—yes, a sense of honour," she insisted, as he threw back his head and laughed. "What do you think might be my reason for concealing the will—if I did conceal it?"

"The answer seems obvious. Why does the wild ass forage with a strange herd, or the pig put his feet in the trough? Not for his neighbour's gain, Madame, not in a thousand years."

"Monsieur, I have never been spoken to so coarsely. I am a blacksmith's daughter, and I have heard rough men talk in my day, but I have never heard a man—of my own race at least—so rude to a woman. But I am here not for my own sake; I will not go till I have said and done all I have come to say and do. Will you listen to me, Monsieur?"

"I have made my charges—answer them. Disprove this theft"—he held up the will—"of concealment, and enjoyment of property not your own, and then ask of me that politeness which makes so beautiful stable and forge at Pontiac."

"Monsieur, you cannot think that the will was concealed for profit, for the value of the Seigneury of Pontiac. I can earn two such seigneuries in one year, Monsieur."

"Nevertheless you do not."

"For the same reason that I did not bring or send that will to you when I found it, Monsieur. And for that same reason I have come to ask you not to take advantage of that will."

He was about to interpose angrily, but she continued: "Whatever the rental may be that you in justice feel should be put upon the Seigneury, I will pay—from the hour my husband entered on the property, its heir as he believed. Put such rental on the property, do not disturb Monsieur Racine in his position as it is, and I will double that rental."

"Do not think, Madame, that I am as avaricious as you."

"Is it avaricious to offer double the worth of the rental?"

"There is the title and distinction. You married a mad nobody; you wish to retain an honour that belongs to me."

"I am asking it for my husband's sake, not my own, believe me, Monsieur."

"And what do you expect me to do for his sake, Madame?"

"What humanity would suggest. Ah, I know what you would say: he tried to kill you; he made you fight him. But, Monsieur, he has repented of that. He is ill, he is—crippled, he cherishes the Seigneury beyond its worth a thousand times."

"He cherishes it at my expense. So, you must not disturb the man who robs you of house and land, and tries to murder you, lest he should be disturbed and not sleep o' nights. Come, Madame, that is too thin."

"He might kill you, but he would not rob you, Monsieur. Do you think that if he knew that will existed, he would be now at the Seigneury, or I here? I know you hate Louis Racine."

"With ample reason."

"You hate him more because he defeated you than because he once tried to kill you. Oh, I do not know the rights or wrongs of that great case at law; I only know that Louis Racine was not the judge or jury, but the avocat only, whose duty it was to do as he did. That he did it the more gladly because he was a Frenchman and you an Englishman, is not his fault or yours either. Louis Racine's people came here two hundred years ago, yours not sixty years ago. You, the great business man, have had practical power which gave you riches. You have sacrificed all for power. Louis Racine has only genius, and no practical power—"

"A dangerous fanatic and dreamer," he interjected.

"A dreamer, if you will, with no practical power, for he never thought of himself, and 'practical power' is usually all self. He dreamed—he gave his heart and soul up for *ideas*. Englishmen do not understand that. Do you not know—you do know—that, had he chosen, he might have been rich too, for his brains would have been of great use to men of practical power like yourself."

She paused. Fournel did not answer, but sat as though reading the will intently.

"Was it strange that he should dream of a French sovereign state here, where his people came and first possessed the land? Can you wonder that this dreamer, when the Seigneury of Pontiac came to him, felt as if a new life were opened up to him, and saw a way to some of his ambitions. They were sad, mistaken ambitions, doomed to failure, but they were also his very heart, which he would empty out gladly for an idea. The Seigneury of Pontiac came to him, and I married him."

"Evidently bent upon wrecking the chances of a great career," interrupted Fournel over the paper.

"But no; I also cared more for ideas than for the sordid things of life. It is in our blood, you see," she was talking with less restraint now, for she saw he was listening, despite assumed indifference—"and Pontiac was dearer to me than all else in the world. Louis Racine belonged there. You—what sort of place would you, an Englishman, have occupied at the Seigneury of Pontiac! What kind—"

He got suddenly to his feet. He was a man of strange whims and vanities, and his resentment at his exclusion from the Seigneury of Pontiac had become a fixed idea. He had hugged the thought of its possession before M. de la Rivière died, as a man humbly born prides himself on the distinguished lineage of his wife. His great schemes were completed, he was a rich man, and he had pictured himself retiring to this Seigneury, a peaceful and practical figure, living out his days in a refined repose which his earlier life had never known. She had touched the raw nerves of his secret vanity.

"What kind of Seigneur would I make, eh? What sort of figure would I cut in Pontiac!" He laughed loudly. "By heaven, Madame, you shall see! I did not move against his outrage and assault, but I will move to purpose now. For you and he shall leave there in disgrace before another week goes round. I have you both in my 'practical power,' and I will squeeze satisfaction out of you. He is a ruffianly interloper, and you, Madame, the law would call by another name."

She got quickly to her feet and came a step nearer to him. Leaning a hand on the table, she bent towards him slightly. Something seemed to possess her that transfigured her face, and gave it a sense of power and confidence. Her eyes fixed themselves steadily on him.

"Monsieur," she said, "you may call me what you will, and I will bear it, for you have been sorely injured. You are angry because I seemed to think an Englishman was not fitted to be Seigneur of Pontiac. We French are a people of sentiments and ideas; we make idols of trifles, and we die for fancies. We dream, we have shrines for memories. These things you despise. You would give us justice and make us rich by what you call progress. Monsieur, that is not enough. We are not born to appreciate you. Our hearts are higher than our heads, and, under a flag that conquered us, they cling together. Was it strange that I should think Louis Racine better suited to be Seigneur at Pontiac?"

She paused as though expecting him to answer, but he only looked inquiringly at her, and she continued "My husband used you ill, but he is no interloper. He took what the law gave him, what has been in his family for over two hundred years. Monsieur, it has meant more to him than a hundred times greater honour could to you. When his trouble came, when—" she paused, as though it was difficult to speak—"when the other—legacy—of his family descended on him, that Seigneury became to him the one compensation of his life. By right of it only could he look the world in the face—or me."

She stopped suddenly, for her voice choked her. "Will you please continue?" said Fournel, opening and shutting the will in his hand, and looking at her with a curious new consideration.

"Fame came to me as his trouble came to him. It was hard for him to go among men, but, ah, can you think how he dreaded the day when I should return to Pontiac! . . . I will tell you the whole truth, Monsieur." She drew herself up proudly. "I loved—Louis. He came into my heart with its first great dream, and before life—the business of life—really began. He was one with the best part of me, the girlhood in me which is dead."

Fournel rose and in a low voice said: "Will you not sit down?" He motioned to a chair.

She shook her head. "Ah no, please! Let me say all quickly and while I have the courage. I loved him, and he loved and loves me. I love that love in which I married him, and I love his love for me. It is indestructible, because it is in the fibre of my life. It has nothing to do with ugliness or beauty, or fortune or misfortune, or shame or happiness, or sin or holiness. When it becomes part of us, it must go on in one form or another, but it cannot die. It lives in breath and song and thought and work and words. That is the wonder of it, the pity of it, and the joy of it. Because it is so, because love would shield the beloved from itself if need be, and from all the terrors of the world at any cost, I have done what I have done. I did it at cost of my honour, but it was for his sake; at the price of my peace, but to spare him. Ah, Monsieur, the days of life are not many for him: his shame and his futile aims are killing him. The clouds will soon close over, and his vexed brain and body will be still. To spare him the last turn of the wheel of torture, to give him the one bare honour left him yet a little while, I have given up my work of life to comfort him. I concealed, I stole, if you will, the document you hold. And, God help me! I would do it again and yet again, if I lost my soul for ever, Monsieur. Monsieur, I know that in his madness he would have killed you, but it was his suffering, not a bad heart, that made him do it. Do a sorrowful woman a great kindness and spare him, Monsieur."

She had held the man motionless and staring. When she ended, he got to his feet and came near to her. There was a curious look in his face, half struggle, half mysterious purpose. "The way is easy to a hundred times as much," he said, in a low meaning voice, and his eyes boldly held hers. "You are doing a chivalrous sort of thing that only a woman would do—for duty; do something for another reason: for what a woman would do—for the blood of youth that is in her." He reached out a hand to lay it on her arm. "Ask of me what you will, if you but put your hand in mine and—"

"Monsieur," she said, pale and gasping, "do you think so ill of me then? Do I seem to you like—!" She turned away, her eyes dry and burning, her body trembling with shame.

"You are here alone with me at night," he persisted. "It would not be easy to—"

"Death would be easy, Monsieur," she said calmly and coldly. "My husband tried to kill you. You would do—ah, but let me pass!" she said, with a sudden fury. "You—if you were a million times richer, if you could ruin me for ever, do you think—"

"Hush, Madame," he said, with a sudden change of voice and a manner all reverence. "I do not think. I spoke only to hear you speak in reply: only to know to the uttermost what you were, Madame," he added, in a shaking voice, "I did not know that such a woman lived. Madame, I could have sworn there was none in the world." Then in a quicker, huskier note he added: "Eighteen years ago a woman nearly spoiled my life. She was as beautiful as you, but her heart was tainted. Since then I have never believed in any woman—never till now. I have said that all were purchasable—at a price. I unsay that now. I have not believed in any one—"

"Oh, Monsieur!" she said, with a quick impulsive gesture towards him, and her face lighting with sympathy.

"I was struck too hard—"

She touched his arm and said gently: "Some are hurt in one way and some in another; all are hurt some time, but—"

"You shall have your way," he interrupted, and moved apart.

"Ah, Monsieur, Monsieur, it is a noble act!—" she hurriedly rejoined, then with a sudden cry rushed towards him, for he was lighting the will at the flame of a candle near him.

"But no, no, no, you shall not do it," she cried. "I only asked it for while he lives—ah!"

She collapsed with a cry of despair, for he had held the flaming paper above her reach, and its ashes were now scattering on the floor.

"You will let me give you some wine?" he said quietly, and poured out a glassful.

CHAPTER NINE

The Biter Bitten

Madelinette was faint, and, sitting down, she drank the wine feebly, then leaned her head against the back of the chair, her face turned from Fournel.

"Forgive me, if you can," he said. "You have this to comfort you, that if friendship is a boon in this world you have an honest friend in George Fournel."

She made a gesture of assent with her hand, but she did not speak. Tears were stealing quietly down her cold face. For a moment so, in silence, and then she rose to her feet, and pulled down over her face the veil she wore. She was about to hold out her hand to him to say good-bye, when there was a noise without, a knocking at the door, then it was flung open, and Tardif, intoxicated, entered followed by two constables, with Fournel's servant vainly protesting.

"Here she is," Tardif said to the officers of the law, pointing to Madelinette. "It was her set the fellow on to shoot me. I had the will she stole from him," he added, pointing to Fournel.

Distressed as Madelinette was, she was composed and ready.

"The man was dismissed my employ—" she began, but Fournel interposed.

"What is this I hear about shooting and a will?" he said sternly.

"What will!" cried Tardif. "The will I brought you from Pontiac, and Madame there followed, and her servant shot me. The will I brought you, M'sieu'. The will leaving the Manor of Pontiac to you!"

Fournel turned as though with sudden anger to the officers. "You come here—you enter my house to interfere with a guest of mine, on the charge of a drunken scoundrel like this! What is this talk of wills! The vapourings of his drunken brain. The Seigneury of Pontiac belongs to Monsieur Racine, and but three days since Madame here dismissed this fellow for pilfering and other misdemeanours. As for shooting—the man is a liar, and—"

"Ah, do you deny that I came to you?—" began Tardif.

"Constables," said Fournel, "I give this fellow in charge. Take him to gaol, and I will appear at court against him when called upon."

Tardif's rage choked him. He tried to speak once or twice, then began to shriek an imprecation at Fournel; but the constables clapped hands on his mouth, and dragged him out of the room and out of the house.

Fournel saw him safely out, then returned to Madelinette. "Do not fear for the fellow. A little gaol will do him good. I will see to it that he gives no trouble, Madame," he said. "You may trust me."

"I do trust you, Monsieur," Madelinette answered quietly. "I pray that you may be right, and that—"

"It will all come out right," he firmly insisted.

"Will you ask for Madame Marie?" she said. Then, with a smile: "We will go happier than we came."

As she and Madame Marie passed from the house, Fournel shook Madelinette's hand warmly, and said: " 'All's well that ends well.'"

" 'That ends well!' " answered Madelinette, with a sorrowful questioning in her voice.

"We will make it so," he rejoined, and then they parted.

CHAPTER TEN

The Door That Would Not Open

The old Manor House of Pontiac was alive with light and merriment. It was the early autumn; not cool enough for the doors and windows to be shut, but cool enough to make dancing a pleasure, and to give spirit to the gaiety that filled the old house. The occasion was a notable one for Pontiac. An address of congratulation and appreciation and a splendid gift of silver had been brought to the Manor from the capital by certain high officials of the Government and the Army, representing the people of the Province. At first Madelinette had shrunk from the honour to be done her, and had so written to certain quarters whence the movement had proceeded; but a letter had come to her which had changed her mind. This letter was signed *George Fournel*. Fournel had a right to ask a favour of her; and one that was to do her honour seemed the least that she might grant. He had suffered much at Louis' hands; he had forborne much; and by an act of noble forgiveness and generosity, had left Louis undisturbed in an honour which was not his, and the enjoyment of an estate to which he had no claim. He had given much, suffered much, and had had nothing in return save her measureless and voiceless gratitude. Friendship she could give him; but it was a silent friendship, an incompanionable friendship, founded upon a secret and chivalrous act. He was in Quebec and she in Pontiac; and since that day when he had burned the will before her eyes she had not seen him. She had heard from him but twice; once to tell her that she need have no fear of Tardif, and again, when he urged her to accept the testimonial and the gift to be offered by her grateful fellow-citizens.

The deputation—distinguished and important—had been received by the people of Pontiac with the flaunting of flags, playing of bands, and every demonstration of delight. The honour done to Madelinette was an honour done to Pontiac, and Pontiac had never felt itself so important. It realised that this kind of demonstration was less expensive, and less dangerous, than sedition, privy conspiracy, and rebellion. The vanity of the habitants could be better exercised in applauding Madelinette and in show of welcome to the great men of the land, than in cultivating a dangerous patriotism under the leadership of Louis Racine. Temptations to conspiracy had been few since the day George Fournel, wounded and morose, left the Manor House secretly one night, and carried back to Quebec his resentment and his injuries. Treasonable gossip filtered no longer from doorway to doorway; carbines were not to be had for a song; no more nightly drills and weekly meetings gave a spice of great expectations to their life. Their Seigneur, silent, and pale, and stooped, lived a life apart. If he walked through the town, it was with bitter, abstracted eyes that took little heed of their presence. If he drove, his horses travelled like the wind. At Mass, he looked at no one, saw no one, and, as it would seem, heard no one.

But Madelinette—she was the Madelinette of old, simple, gracious, kind, with a smile here and a kind word there: a little child to be caressed or an old woman to be comforted; the sick to be fed and doctored; the poor to be helped; the idle to be rebuked with a persuasive smile; the angry to be coaxed by a humorous word; the evil to be reproved by a fearless friendliness; the spiteful to be hushed by a still, commanding presence. She never seemed to remember that she was the daughter of old Joe Lajeunesse the blacksmith, yet she never seemed to forget it. She was the wife of the Seigneur, and she was the daughter of the smithy-man too. She sat in the smithy-man's doorway with her hand in his; and she sat at the Manor table with its silver glitter, and its antique garnishings, with as real an unconsciousness.

Her influence seemed to pierce far and wide. The Curé and the Avocat adored her; and the proudest, happiest moment of their lives was when they sat at the Manor table, or, in the sombre drawing-room, watched her give it light and grace and charm, and fill their hearts with the piercing delight of her song. So her life had gone on; to the outward world serene and happy, full of simplicity, charity, and good works. What it was in reality no one could know, not even herself. Since the day when Louis had tried to kill George Fournel, life had been a different thing for them both. On her part she had been deeply hurt; wounded beyond repair. He had failed her from every vital stand-point, he had not fulfilled one hope she had ever had of him. But she laid the blame not at his door; she rather shrank with inner bitterness from the cynical cruelty of nature, which, in deforming the body, with a merciless cruelty had deformed a noble mind. These things were between her and her inmost soul.

To Louis she was ever the same, affectionate, gentle, and unselfish; but her stronger soul ruled him without his knowledge, commanded his perturbed spirit into the abstracted quiet and bitter silence wherein he lived, and which she sought to cheer by a thousand happy devices. She did not let him think that she was giving up anything for him; no word or act of hers could have suggested to him the sacrifices she had made. He knew them, still he did not know them in their fulness; he was grateful, but his gratitude did not compass the splendid self-effacing devotion with which she denied herself the glorious career that had lain before her. Morbid and self-centred, he could not understand. Since her return from Quebec she had sought to give a little touch of gaiety to their life, and she had not the heart to interfere with his constant insistence on the little dignities of the position of Seigneur, ironical as they all were in her eyes. She had sacrificed everything; and since another also had sacrificed himself to give her husband the honours and estate he possessed, the game should be delicately played to the unseen end.

So it had gone on until the coming of the deputation with the testimonial and the gift. She had proposed the gaieties of the occasion to Louis with so simple a cheerfulness, that he had no idea of the torture it meant to her; no realisation of how she would be brought face to face with the life that she had given up for his sake. But neither he nor she was aware of one thing, that the beautiful embossed address contained an appeal to her to return to the world of song which she had renounced, to go forth once more and contribute to the happiness of humanity.

When, therefore, in the drawing-room of the Manor, the address was read to her, and this appeal rang upon her ears, she felt herself turn dizzy and faint: her whole life seemed to reel backwards to all she had lost, and the tyranny of the present bore down upon her with a cruel weight. It needed all her courage and all her innate strength to rule herself to composure. For an instant the people in the room were a confused mass, floating away into a blind distance. She heard, however, the quick breathing of the Seigneur beside her, and it called her back to an active and necessary confidence.

With a smile she received the address, and, turning, handed it to Louis, smiling at him too with a winning duplicity, for which she might never have to ask forgiveness in this world or the next. Then she turned and spoke. Eloquently, simply, she gave out her thanks for the gift of silver and the greater gift of kind words; and said that in her quiet life, apart from that active world of the stage, where sorrow and sordid experience went hand in hand with song, where the delights of home were sacrificed to the applause of the world, she would cherish their gift as a reward that she might have earned, had she chosen the public instead of the private way of life. They had told her of the paths of glory, but she was walking the homeward way.

Thus deftly, and without strain, and with an air of happiness even, did she set aside the words and the appeal which had created a storm in her soul. A few moments afterwards, as the old house rang to the laughter of old and young, with dancing well begun, no one would have thought that the Manor of Pontiac was not the home of peace and joy. Even Louis himself, who had had his moments of torture and suspicion when the appeal was read, was now in a kind of happy reaction. He moved about among the guests with less abstraction and more cheerfulness than he had shown for months. He carried in his hand the address which Madelinette had handed him. Again and again he showed it to eager guests.

Suddenly, as he was about to fold it up for the last time and carry it to the library, he saw the name of George Fournel among the signatures. Stunned, dumfounded, he left the room. George Fournel, whom he had tried to kill, had signed this address of congratulation to his wife! Was it Fournel's intention thus to show that he had forgiven and forgotten? It was not like the man to either forgive or forget. What did it mean? He left the house buried in morbid speculation, and involuntarily made his way to a little hut of two rooms which he had built in the Seigneury grounds. Here it was he read and wrote, here he had spent moody hours alone, day after day, for months past. He was not aware that someone left the crowd about the house and followed him. Arrived at the hut, he entered and shut the door; lighted candles, and spread the embossed parchment out before him upon the table. As he stood looking at it, he heard the door open behind him. Tardif stood before him.

The face of Tardif had an evil hunted look. Before the astonished and suspicious Seigneur had chance to challenge him, he said in a low insolent tone:

"Good evening, M'sieu'! Fine doings at the Manor—eh?"

"What are you doing at the Manor, and what are you doing here?" asked the Seigneur, scanning the face of the man closely; for there was a look in it he did not understand.

"I have as much right to be here as you, M'sieu'."

"You have no right at all to be here. You were dismissed your place by the mistress of this Manor."

"There is no mistress of this Manor."

"Madame Racine dismissed you."

"And I dismissed Madame Racine," answered the man with a sneer.

"You are training for the horsewhip. You forget that, as Seigneur, I have power to give you summary punishment."

"You haven't power to do anything at all, M'sieu'!" The Seigneur started. He thought the remark had reference to his physical disability. His fingers itched to take the creature by the throat, and choke the tongue from his mouth. Before he could speak, the man continued with a half-drunken grimace:

"You, with your tributes, and your courts, and your body-guards! Bah! You'd have a gibbet if you could, wouldn't you? You with your rebellion and your tinpot honours! A puling baby could conspire as well as you. And all the world laughing at you—*v la*!"

"Get out of this room and take your feet from my Manor, Tardif," said the Seigneur with a deadly quietness, "or it will be the worse for you."

"Your Manor—*pish*." The man laughed a hateful laugh. "Your Manor? You haven't any Manor. You haven't anything but what you carry on your back."

A flush passed swiftly over the Seigneur's face, then left it cold and white, and the eyes shone fiery in his head. He felt some shameful meaning in the man's words, beyond this gross reference to his deformity.

"I am Seigneur of this Manor, and you have taken wages from me, and eaten my bread, slept under my roof, and—"

"I've no more eaten your bread and slept under your roof than you have. *Pish!* You were living then on another man's fortune, now you're living on what your wife earns."

The Seigneur did not understand yet. But there was a strange light of suspicion in his eyes, a nervous rage knotting his forehead.

"My land and my earnings are my own, and I have never lived on another man's fortune. If you mean that the late Seigneur made a will—that *canard*[17]—"

"It was no canard." Tardif laughed hatefully. "There was a will right enough."

"Where is it? I've heard that fool's gossip before."

"Where is it? Ask your wife; she knows. Ask your loving Tardif, he knows."

"Where is the will, Tardif?" asked the Seigneur in a voice that, in his own ears, seemed to come from an infinite distance; to Tardif's ears it was merely tuneless and harsh.

"In M'sieu' Fournel's pocket, or Madame's. What's the difference? The price is the same, and you keep your eyes shut and play the Seigneur, and eat and drink what they give you just the same."

Now the Seigneur understood. His eyes went blind for a moment, and his hands twitched convulsively on the embossed address he had been rolling and unrolling. A terror, a shame, a dreadful cruelty entered into him, but he was still and numb, and his tongue was thick. He spoke heavily.

"Tell me all," he said. "You shall be well paid."

"I don't want your money. I want to see you squirm. I want to see her put where she deserves. Bah! Do you think Fournel forgave you for putting his feet in his shoes, and for that case at law, for nothing? Why should he? He hated you, and you hated him. His name's on that paper in your hand among all the rest. Do you think he eats

---

[17] A untrue story or rumour.

humble pie and crawls to Madame and lets you stay here for nothing?"

The Seigneur was painfully quiet and intent, yet his brain was like some great lens, refracting and magnifying things to monstrous proportions.

"A will was found?" he asked.

"By Madame in the library. She left it where she found it—behind the picture over the Louis Seize table. The day you dismissed me, I saw her at the cupboard. I found the will and started with it to M'sieu' Fournel. She followed. You remember when she went—eh? On business—and such business! she and Havel and the old slut Marie. You remember, eh; Louis?" he added with unnamable insolence. The Seigneur inclined his head. "*V là!* they followed me, overtook me, and Havel shot me in the wrist. See there!"—he held out his wrist. The Seigneur nodded. "But I got to Fournel's first. I put the will into his hands.

"I told him Madame Madelinette was following. Then I went to bring the constables to his house to arrest her when he had finished with her." He laughed a brutal laugh, which deepened the strange glittering look in Louis' eyes. "When I came an hour later, she was there. But—now you shall see what stuff they are both made of! He laughed at me, said I had lied; that there was no will; that I was a thief; and had me locked up in gaol. For a month I was in gaol without trial. Then one day I was let out without trial. His servant met me and brought me to his house. He gave me money and told me to leave the country. If I didn't, I would be arrested again for trying to shoot Havel, and for blackmail. They could all swear me off my feet and into prison—what was I to do! I took the money and went. But I came back to have my revenge. I could cut their hearts out and eat them."

"You are drunk," said the Seigneur quietly. "You don't know what you're saying."

"I'm not drunk. I'm always trying to get drunk now. I couldn't have come here if I hadn't been drinking. I couldn't have told you the truth, if I hadn't been drinking. But I'm sober enough to know that I've done for him and for her! And I'm even with you too—*bah!* Did you think she cared a fig for you? She's only waiting till you die. Then she'll go to her lover. He's a man of life and limb. You—*pish!* a hunchback, that all the world laughs at, a worm—" he turned towards the door laughing hideously, his evil face gloating. "You've not got a stick or stone. *She*"—jerking a finger towards the house— "she earns what you eat, she—"

It was the last word he ever spoke, for, with a low terrible cry, the Seigneur snatched up a knife from the table and sprang upon him, catching him by the throat. Once, twice, thrice, the knife went home, and the ruffian collapsed under it with one loud cry. Not letting go his grasp of the dying man's collar, the Seigneur dragged him across the floor, and, opening the door of the small inner room, pulled him inside. For a moment he stood beside the body, panting, then he went to the other room and, bringing a candle, looked at the dead thing in silence. Presently he stooped, held the candle to the wide-staring eyes, then felt the heart. "He is gone," he said in an even voice. Stooping for the knife he had dropped on the floor, he laid it on the body. He looked at his hands. There was one spot of blood on his fingers. He wiped it off with his handkerchief, then blowing out the light, he calmly opened the door of the hut, locked it, went out, and moved on slowly towards the house.

As he left the hut he was conscious that someone was moving under the trees by the window, but his mind was not concerned with things outside himself and the one other thing left for him to do.

He entered the house and went in search of Madelinette. When he reached the drawing-room, surrounded by eager listeners, she was beginning to sing. Her bearing was eager and almost tremulous, for, with this crowd round her and in the flush of this gaiety and excitement, there was something of that exhilarating air that greets the singer upon the stage. Her eyes were shining with a look, half-sorrowful, half-triumphant. Within the past half-hour she had overcome herself; she had fought down the blind, wild rebellion that, for one moment as it were, had surged up in her heart. She was proud and glad, and piteous and triumphant and deeply womanly all at once.

Going to the piano she had looked round for Louis, but he was not visible. She smiled to herself, however, for she knew that her singing would bring him—he worshipped it. Her heart was warm towards him, because of that moment when she rebelled and was hard at soul. She played her own accompaniment, and he was hidden from her by the piano as she sang—sang more touchingly and more humanly, if not more artistically, than she had ever done in her life. The old art was not so perfect, perhaps, but there was in the voice all that she had learned and loved and suffered and hoped. When she rose from the piano to a storm of applause, and saw the shining faces and tearful eyes round her, her own eyes filled with tears. These people—most of them—had known and loved her since she was a child, and loved her still without envy or any taint. Her father was standing near, and with smiling face she caught from his hand the handkerchief with which he was mopping his eyes, and kissed him, saying:

"I learned that from the tunes you played on your anvil, dear smithy-man."

Then she turned again to look for Louis. Near the door she saw him, and with so strange a face, so wild a look, that, unheeding eager requests to sing again, she responded to the gesture he made, made her way through the crowd to the hall-way, and followed him up the stairs, and to the little boudoir beside her bedroom. As she entered and shut the door, a low sound like a moan broke from him. She went quickly to lay a hand upon his arm, but he waved her back. "What is it, Louis?" she asked, in a bewildered voice. "Where is the will?" he said.

"Where is the will, Louis," she repeated after him mechanically, staring at his face, ghostly in the moonlight.

"The will you found behind the picture in the library."

"O Louis!" she cried, and made a gesture of despair. "O Louis!"

"You found it, and Tardif stole it and took it to Quebec."

"Yes, Louis, but Louis—ah, what is the matter, dear! I cannot bear that look in your face. What is the matter, Louis?"

"Tardif took it to Fournel, and you followed. And I have been living in another man's house, on another's bread—"

"O Louis, no—no—no! Our money has paid for all."

"Your money, Madelinette!" His voice rose.

"Ah, don't speak like that! See, Louis. It can make no difference. How you have found out I do not know, but it can make no difference. I did not want you to know—you loved the Seigneury so. I concealed the will; Tardif found it, as you say. But, Louis, dear, it is all right. Monsieur Fournel would not take the place, and—and I have bought it."

She told her falsehood fearlessly. This man's trouble, this man's peace, if she might but win it, was the purpose of her life.

"Tardif said that—he said that you—that you and Fournel—"

She read his meaning in his tone, and shrank back in terror, then with a flush, straightened herself, and took a step towards him.

"It was natural that you should not care for a hunchback like me," he continued, "but—"

"Louis!" she cried, in a voice of anguish and reproach.

"But I did not doubt you. I believed in you when he said it, as I believe in you now when you stand there like that. I know what you have done for me—"

"I pleaded with Monsieur Fournel, knowing how you loved the Seigneury—pleaded and offered to pay three times the price—"

"*Yourself* would have been a hundred million times the price. Ah, I know you, Madelinette—I know you now! I have been selfish, but I see all now. Now when all is over—" he seemed listening to noises with out—"I see what you have done for me. I know how you have sacrificed all for me—all but honour—all but honour," he added, a wild fire in his eyes, a trembling seizing him. "Your honour is yours forever. I say so. I say so, and I have proved it. Kiss me, Madelinette—kiss me once," he added, in a quick whisper.

"My poor, poor Louis!" she said, laid a soothing hand upon his arm, and leaned towards him. He snatched her to his breast, and kissed her twice in a very agony of joy, then let her go. He listened for an instant to the growing noise without, then said in a hoarse voice:

"Now, I will tell you, Madelinette. They are coming for me—don't you hear them? They are coming to take me; but they shall not have me. They shall not have me—" he glanced to a little door that led into a bath-room at his right.

"Louis—Louis!" she said in a sudden fright, for though his words seemed mad, a strange quiet sanity was in all he did. "What have you done? Who are coming?" she asked in agony, and caught him by the arm.

"I killed Tardif. He is there in the hut in the garden—dead! I was seen, and they are coming to take me."

With a cry she ran to the door that led into the hall, and locked it. She listened, then turned her face to Louis.

"You killed him!" she gasped. "Louis! Louis!" Her face was like ashes.

"I stabbed him to death. It was all I could do, and I did it. He slandered you. I went mad, and did it. Now—"

There was a knocking at the door, and a voice calling—a peremptory voice.

"There is only one way," he said. "They shall not take me. I will not be dragged to gaol for crowds to jeer at. I will not be sent to the scaffold, to your shame."

He ran to the door of the bath-room and flung it open. "If my life is to pay the price, then—!"

She came blindly towards him, stretching out her hands.

"Louis! Louis!" was all that she could say.

He caught her hands and kissed them, then stepped swiftly back into the little bath-room, and locked the door, as the door of the room she was in was burst open, and two constables and a half-dozen men crowded into the room.

She stood with her back to the bath-room door, panting, and white, and anguished, and her ears strained to the terrible thing inside the place behind her.

The men understood, and came towards her. "Stand back," she said. "You shall not have him. You shall not have him. Ah, don't you hear? He is dying—O God, O God!" she cried, with tearless eyes and upturned face—"Ah, let it be soon! Ah, let him die soon!"

The men stood abashed before her agony. Behind the little door where she stood there was a muffled groaning. She trembled, but her arms were spread out before the door as though on a cross, and her lips kept murmuring: "O God, let him die! Let him die! Oh spare him agony!"

Suddenly she stood still and listened—listened, with staring eyes that saw nothing. In the room men shrank back, for they knew that death was behind the little door, and that they were in the presence of a sorrow greater than death.

Suddenly she turned upon them with a gesture of piteous triumph and said:

"You cannot have him now."

Then she swayed and fell forward to the floor as the Curé and George Fournel entered the room. The Curé hastened to her side and lifted up her head.

George Fournel pushed the men back who would have entered the bath-room, and himself, bursting the door open, entered. Louis lay dead upon the floor. He turned to the constables.

"As she said, you cannot have him now. You have no right here. Go. I had a warning from the man he killed. I knew there would be trouble. But I have come too late," he added bitterly.

* * * *

An hour later the house was as still as the grave. Madame Marie sat with the doctor beside the bed of her dear mistress, and in another room, George Fournel, with the Avocat, kept watch beside the body of the Seigneur of Pontiac. The face of the dead man was as peaceful as that of a little child.

At ninety years of age, the present Seigneur of Pontiac, one Baron Fournel, lives in the Manor House left him by Madelinette Lajeunesse the great singer, when she died a quarter of a century ago. For thirty years he followed her from capital to capital of Europe and America to hear her sing; and to this day he talks of her in language more French than English in its ardour. Perhaps that is because his heart beats in sympathy with the Frenchmen he once disdained.

THE ABSURD ROMANCE OF P'TITE LOUISON

The five brothers lived with Louison, three miles from Pontiac, and Medallion came to know them first through having sold them, at an auction, a slice of an adjoining farm. He had been invited to their home, intimacy had grown, and afterwards, stricken with a severe illness, he had been taken into the household and kept there till he was well again. The night of his arrival, Louison, the sister, stood with a brother on either hand—Octave and Florian—and received him with a courtesy more stately than usual, an expression of the reserve and modesty of her single state. This maidenly dignity was at all times shielded by the five brothers, who treated her with a constant and reverential courtesy. There was something signally suggestive in their homage, and Medallion concluded at last that it was paid not only to the sister, but to something that gave her great importance in their eyes.

He puzzled long, and finally decided that Louison had a romance. There was something which suggested it in the way they said "P'tite Louison"; in the manner they avoided all gossip regarding marriages and marriage-feasting; in the way they deferred to her on questions of etiquette (as, for instance, Should the eldest child be given the family name of the wife or a Christian name from her husband's family?). And P'tite Louison's opinion was accepted instantly as final, with satisfied nods on the part of all the brothers, and whispers of "How clever! how adorable!"

P'tite Louison affected never to hear these remarks, but looked complacently straight before her, stirring the spoon in her cup, or benignly passing the bread and butter. She was quite aware of the homage paid to her, and she gracefully accepted the fact that she was an object of interest.

Medallion had not the heart to laugh at the adoration of the brothers, or at the outlandish sister, for, though she was angular, and sallow, and thin, and her hands were large and red, there was a something deep in her eyes, a curious quality in her carriage commanding respect. She had ruled these brothers, had been worshipped by them, for near half a century, and the romance they had kept alive had produced a grotesque sort of truth and beauty in the admiring "P'tite Louison"—an affectionate name for her greatness, like "The Little Corporal" for Napoleon. She was not little, either, but above the middle height, and her hair was well streaked with grey.

Her manner towards Medallion was not marked by any affectation. She was friendly in a kind, impersonal way, much as a nurse cares for a patient, and she never relaxed a sort of old-fashioned courtesy, which might have been trying in such close quarters, were it not for the real simplicity of the life and the spirit and lightness of their race. One night Florian—there were Florian and Octave and Felix and Isidore and Emile—the eldest, drew Medallion aside from the others, and they walked together by the river. Florian's air suggested confidence and mystery, and soon, with a voice of hushed suggestion, he told Medallion the romance of P'tite Louison. And each of the brothers at different times during the next fortnight did the same, differing scarcely at all in details, or choice of phrase or meaning, and not at all in general facts and essentials. But each, as he ended, made a different exclamation.

"*Voilà!* so sad, so wonderful! She keeps the ring—dear P'tite Louison!" said Florian, the eldest.

"*Alors!* she gives him a legacy in her will! Sweet P'tite Louison," said Octave.

"*Mais!* the governor and the archbishop admire her—P'tite Louison," said Felix, nodding confidently at Medallion.

"*Bien!* you should see the linen and the petticoats!" said Isidore, the humorous one of the family. "He was great—she was an angel— P'tite Louison!"

"*Attends!* what love—what history—what passion!—the perfect P'tite Louison!" cried Emile, the youngest, the most sentimental. "Ah, Molière!" he added, as if calling on the master to rise and sing the glories of this daughter of romance.

Isidore's tale was after this fashion:

"I ver' well remember the first of it; and the last of it—who can tell? He was an actor—oh, so droll, that! Tall, ver' smart, and he play in theatre at Montreal. It is in the winter. P'tite Louison visit Montreal. She walk past the theatre and, as she go by, she slip on the snow and fall. Out from a door with a jomp come M'sieu' Hadrian, and pick her up. And when he see the purty face of P'tite Louison, his eyes go all fire, and he clasp her hand to his breast.

"'Mademoiselle! Mademoiselle!' he say, 'we must meet again!'

"She thank him and hurry away quick. Next day we are on the river, and P'tite Louison try to do the Dance of the Blue Fox on the ice. While she do it, someone come up swift, and catch her hand and say: 'Ma'm'selle, let's do it together'—like that! It take her breath away. It is M'sieu' Hadrian. He not seem like the other men she know; but he have a sharp look, he is smooth in the face, and he smile kind like a woman. P'tite Louison, she give him her hand, and they run away, and every one stop to look. It is a gran' sight. M'sieu' Hadrian laugh, and his teeth shine, and the ladies say things of him, and he tell P'tite Louison that she look ver' fine, and walk like a queen. I am there that day, and I see all, and I think it dam good. I say: 'That P'tite Louison, she beat them all'—I am only twelve year old then. When M'sieu' Hadrian leave, he give her two seats for the theatre, and we go. Bagosh! that is grand thing that play, and M'sieu' Hadrian, he is a prince; and when he say to his minister, 'But no, my lord, I will marry out of my star, and where my heart go, not as the State wills,' he look down at P'tite Louison, and she go all red, and some of the women look at her, and there is a whisper all roun'.

"Nex' day he come to the house where we stay, but the Curé come also pretty soon and tell her she must go home—he say an actor is not good company. Never mind. And so we come out home. Well, what you think? Nex' day M'sieu' Hadrian come, too, and we have dam good time—Florian, Octave, Felix, Emile, they all sit and say bully-good to him all the time. Holy, what fine stories he tell! And he talk about P'tite Louison, and his eyes get wet, and Emile he say his prayers to him—bagosh! yes, I think. Well, at last, what you guess? M'sieu' he come and come, and at last one day, he say that he leave Montreal and go to New York, where he get a good place in a big theatre—his time in Montreal is finish. So he speak to Florian and say he want marry P'tite Louison, and he say, of course, that he is not marry and he have money. But he is a Protestan', and the Curé at first ver' mad, bagosh!

"But at las' when he give a hunder' dollars to the Church, the Curé say yes. All happy that way for while. P'tite Louison, she get ready quick— *sapré,*[18] what fine things had she—and it is all to be done in a week, while the theatre in New York wait for M'sieu'. He sit there with us, and play on the fiddle, and sing songs, and act plays, and help Florian in the barn, and Octave to mend the fence, and the Curé to fix the grape-vines on his wall. He show me and Emile how to play sword-sticks; and he pick flowers and fetch them to P'tite Louison, and teach her how to make an omelette and a salad like the chef of the Louis Quinze Hotel, so he say. Bagosh, what a good time we have! But first one, then another, he get a choke-throat when he think that P'tite Louison go to leave us, and the more we try, the more we are bagosh fools. And that P'tite Louison, she kiss us hevery one, and say to M'sieu' Hadrian, 'Charles, I love you, but I cannot go.' He laugh at her, and say, '*Voilà!* we will take them all with us,' and P'tite Louison she laugh. That night a thing happen. The Curé come, and he look ver' mad, and he frown and he say to M'sieu' Hadrian before us all, 'M'sieu', you are married.'

"*Sapré!* that P'tite Louison get pale like snow, and we all stan' roun' her close and say to her quick, 'Courage, P'tite Louison!' M'sieu' Hadrian then look at the priest and say: 'No, M'sieu', I was

[18] A "softened" oath, a variation of the French *sacré* or sacred.

married ten years ago; my wife drink and go wrong, and I get divorce. I am free like the wind.'

"'You are not free,' the Curé say quick. 'Once married, married till death. The Church cannot marry you again, and I command Louison to give you up.'

"P'tite Louison stan' like stone. M'sieu' turn to her. 'What shall it be, Louison?' he say. 'You will come with me?'

"'Kiss me, Charles,' she say, 'and tell me good-bye till—till you are free.'

"He look like a madman. 'Kiss me once, Charles,' she say, 'and let me go.'

"And he come to her and kiss her on the lips once, and he say, 'Louison, come with me. I will never give you up.'

"She draw back to Florian. 'Good-bye, Charles,' she say. 'I will wait as long as you will. Mother of God, how hard it is to do right!' she say, and then she turn and leave the room.

"M'sieu' Hadrian, he give a long sigh. 'It was my one chance,' he say. 'Now the devil take it all!' Then he nod and say to the Curé: 'We'll thrash this out at Judgment Day, M'sieu'. I'll meet you there— you and the woman that spoiled me.'

"He turn to Florian and the rest of us, and shake hands, and say: 'Take care of Louison. Thank you. Good-bye.' Then he start towards the door, but stumble, for he look sick. 'Give me a drink,' he say, and begin to cough a little—a queer sort of rattle. Florian give him big drink, and he toss it off-whiff! 'Thank you,' he say, and start again, and we see him walk away over the hill ver' slow—an' he never come back. But every year there come from New York a box of flowers, and every year P'tite Louison send him a 'Merci, Charles, mille fois. Dieu te garde.' It is so every year for twenty-five year."

"Where is he now?" asked Medallion.

Isidore shook his head, then lifted his eyes religiously. "Waiting for Judgment Day and P'tite Louison," he answered.

"Dead!" said Medallion.

"How long?"

"Twenty year."

"But the flowers—the flowers?"

"He left word for them to be sent just the same, and the money for it."

Medallion turned and took off his hat reverently, as if a soul were passing from the world; but it was only P'tite Louison going out into the garden.

"She thinks him living?" he asked gently as he watched Louison.

"Yes; we have no heart to tell her. And then he wish it so. And the flowers kep' coming."

"Why did he wish it so?" Isidore mused a while.

"Who can tell? Perhaps a whim. He was a great actor—ah, yes, sublime!" he said.

Medallion did not reply, but walked slowly down to where P'tite Louison was picking berries. His hat was still off.

"Let me help you, Mademoiselle," he said softly. And henceforth he was as foolish as her brothers.

THE LITTLE BELL OF HONOUR

"*S* *acré baptème!*"

"What did he say?" asked the Little Chemist, stepping from his doorway.

"He cursed his baptism," answered tall Medallion, the English auctioneer, pushing his way farther into the crowd.

"Ah, the pitiful *vaurien!*" [19] said the Little Chemist's wife, shudderingly; for that was an oath not to be endured by anyone who called the Church mother.

The crowd that had gathered at the Four Corners were greatly disturbed, for they also felt the repulsion that possessed the Little Chemist's wife. They babbled, shook their heads, and waved their hands excitedly, and swayed and craned their necks to see the offender.

All at once his voice, mad with rage, was heard above the rest, shouting frenziedly a curse which was a horribly grotesque

---

[19] A scamp or reprobate.

blasphemy upon the name of God. Men who had used that oath in their insane anger had been known to commit suicide out of remorse afterwards.

For a moment there was a painful hush. The crowd drew back involuntarily and left a clear space, in which stood the blasphemer— a middle-sized, athletic fellow, with black beard, thick, waving hair, and flashing brown eyes. His white teeth were showing now in a snarl like a dog's, his cap was on the ground, his hair was tumbled, his hands were twitching with passion, his foot was stamping with fury, and every time it struck the ground a little silver bell rang at his knee—a pretty sylvan sound, in no keeping with the scene. It heightened the distress of the fellow's blasphemy and ungovernable anger. For a man to curse his baptism was a wicked thing; but the other oath was not fit for human ears, and horror held the crowd moveless for a moment.

Then, as suddenly as the stillness came, a low, threatening mumble of voices rose, and a movement to close in on the man was made; but a figure pushed through the crowd, and, standing in front of the man, waved the people back. It was the Curé, the beloved M. Fabre, whose life had been spent among them, whom they obeyed as well as they could, for they were but frail humanity, after all—crude, simple folk, touched with imagination.

"Luc Pomfrette, why have you done this? What provocation had you?"

The Curé's voice was stern and cold, his usually gentle face had become severe, his soft eyes were piercing and determined.

The foot of the man still beat the ground angrily, and the little bell kept tinkling. He was gasping with passion, and he did not answer yet.

"Luc Pomfrette, what have you to say?" asked the Curé again. He motioned back Lacasse, the constable of the parish, who had suddenly appeared with a rusty gun and a more rusty pair of handcuffs.

Still the voyageur did not answer.

The Curé glanced at Lajeunesse the blacksmith, who stood near.

"There was no cause—no," sagely shaking his head said Lajeunesse, "Here stand we at the door of the Louis Quinze in very good humour. Up come the voyageurs, all laughing, and ahead of them is Luc Pomfrette, with the little bell at his knee. Luc, he laugh the same as the rest, and they stand in the door, and the *garçon* bring out the brandy—just a little, but just enough too. I am talking to Henri Beauvin. I am telling him Junie Gauloir have run away with Dicey the Protestant, when all very quick Luc push between me and Henri, jump into the street, and speak like that!"

Lajeunesse looked around, as if for corroboration; Henri and others nodded, and some one said:

"That's true; that's true. There was no cause."

"Maybe it was the drink," said a little hunchbacked man, pushing his way in beside the Curé. "It must have been the drink; there was nothing else—no."

The speaker was Parpon the dwarf, the oddest, in some ways the most foolish, in others the wisest man in Pontiac.

"That is no excuse," said the Curé.

"It is the only one he has, eh?" answered Parpon. His eyes were fixed meaningly on those of Pomfrette.

"It is no excuse," repeated the Curé sternly. "The blasphemy is horrible, a shame and stigma upon Pontiac forever." He looked Pomfrette in the face. "Foul-mouthed and wicked man, it is two years since you took the Blessed Sacrament. Last Easter day you were in a drunken sleep while Mass was being said; after the funeral of your own father you were drunk again. When you went away to the woods you never left a penny for candles, nor for Masses to be said for your father's soul; yet you sold his horse and his little house, and spent the money in drink. Not a cent for a candle, but—"

"It's a lie," cried Pomfrette, shaking with rage from head to foot.

A long horror-stricken "Ah!" broke from the crowd. The Curé's face became graver and colder.

"You have a bad heart," he answered, "and you give Pontiac an evil name. I command you to come to Mass next Sunday, to repent and to hear your penance given from the altar. For until—"

"I'll go to no Mass till I'm carried to it," was the sullen, malevolent interruption.

The Curé turned upon the people.

"This is a blasphemer, an evil-hearted, shameless man," he said. "Until he repents humbly, and bows his vicious spirit to holy Church, and his heart to the mercy of God, I command you to avoid him as you would a plague. I command that no door be opened to him; that no one offer him comfort or friendship; that not even a *bon jour* or a *bon soir* pass between you. He has blasphemed against our Father in heaven; to the Church he is a leper." He turned to Pomfrette. "I pray God that you have no peace in mind or body till your evil life is changed, and your black heart is broken by sorrow and repentance."

Then to the people he said again: "I have commanded you for your souls' sake; see that you obey. Go to your homes. Let us leave the leper—alone." He waved the awed crowd back.

"Shall we take off the little bell?" asked Lajeunesse of the Curé.

Pomfrette heard, and he drew himself together, his jaws shutting with ferocity, and his hand flying to the belt where his voyageur's case-knife hung. The Curé did not see this. Without turning his head towards Pomfrette, he said:

"I have commanded you, my children. Leave the leper alone."

Again he waved the crowd to be gone, and they scattered, whispering to each other; for nothing like this had ever occurred in Pontiac before, nor had they ever seen the Curé with this granite look in his face, or heard his voice so bitterly hard.

He did not move until he had seen them all started homewards from the Four Corners. One person remained beside him—Parpon the dwarf.

"I will not obey you, M'sieu' le Curé," said he. "*I'll* forgive him *before* he repents."

"You will share his sin," answered the Curé sternly.

"No; his punishment, M'sieu'," said the dwarf; and turning on his heel, he trotted to where Pomfrette stood alone in the middle of the road, a dark, morose figure, hatred and a wild trouble in his face.

Already banishment, isolation, seemed to possess Pomfrette, to surround him with loneliness. The very effort he made to be defiant of his fate appeared to make him still more solitary. All at once he thrust a hand inside his red shirt, and, giving a jerk which broke a string tied round his neck, he drew forth a little pad—a flat bag of silk, called an Agnus Dei,[20] worn as a protection and a blessing by the pious, and threw it on the ground. Another little parcel he drew from his belt, and ground it into the dirt with his heel. It contained a woman's hair. Then, muttering, his hands still twitching with savage feeling, he picked up his cap, covered with dirt, put it on, and passed

[20] Latin: Lamb of God.

away down the road towards the river, the little bell tinkling as he went. Those who heard it had a strange feeling, for already to them the man was as if he had some baleful disease, and this little bell told of the passing of a leper.

Yet some one man had worn just such a bell every year in Pontiac. It was the mark of honour conferred upon a voyageur by his fellows, the token of his prowess and his skill. This year Luc Pomfrette had won it, and that very day it had been buckled round his leg with songs and toasts.

For hours Pomfrette walked incessantly up and down the riverbank, muttering and gesticulating, but at last came quietly to the cottage which he shared with Henri Beauvin. Henri had removed himself and his belongings: already the ostracising had begun. He went to the bedroom of old Mme. Burgoyne, his cousin; she also was gone. He went to a little outhouse and called.

For reply there was a scratching at the door. He opened it, and a dog leaped out and upon him. With a fierce fondness he snatched at the dog's collar, and drew the shaggy head to his knee; then as suddenly shoved him away with a smothered oath, and going into the house, shut the door. He sat down in a chair in the middle of the room, and scarcely stirred for half an-hour. At last, with a passionate jerk of the head, he got to his feet, looking about the room in a half-distracted way. Outside, the dog kept running round and round the house, silent, watchful, waiting for the door to open.

As time went by, Luc became quieter, but the look of his face was more desolate. At last he almost ran to the door, threw it open, and called. The dog sprang into the room, went straight to the fireplace, lay down, and with tongue lolling and body panting looked at Pomfrette with blinking, uncomprehending eyes.

Pomfrette went to a cupboard, brought back a bone well covered with meat, and gave it to the dog, which snatched it and began gnawing it, now and again stopping to look up at his master, as one might look at a mountain moving, be aware of something singular, yet not grasp the significance of the phenomenon. At last, worn out, Pomfrette threw himself on his bed, and fell into a sound sleep. When he awoke, it was far into the morning. He lighted a fire in the kitchen, got a "spider," fried himself a piece of pork, and made some tea. There was no milk in the cupboard; so he took a pitcher and walked down the road a few rods to the next house, where lived the village milkman. He knocked, and the door was opened by the milkman's wife. A frightened look came upon her when she saw who it was.

'Non, non.' she said, and shut the door in his face. He stared blankly at the door for a moment, then turned round and stood looking down into the road, with the pitcher in his hand. The milkman's little boy, Maxime, came running round the corner of the house. "Maxime," he said involuntarily and half-eagerly, for he and the lad had been great friends.

Maxime's face brightened, then became clouded; he stood still an instant, and presently, turning round and looking at Pomfrette askance, ran away behind the house, saying: 'Non, non.'

Pomfrette drew his rough knuckles across his forehead in a dazed way; then, as the significance of the thing came home to him, he broke out with a fierce oath, and strode away down the yard and into the road. On the way to his house he met Duclosse the mealman and Garotte the lime-burner.[21] He wondered what they would do.

---

[21] Garotte's profession is to heat limestone to produce lime, used for the creation of mortar.

He could see the fat, wheezy Duclosse hesitate, but the arid, alert Garotte had determination in every motion and look. They came nearer; they were about to pass; there was no sign.

Pomfrette stopped short. "Good-day, lime-burner; good-day, Duclosse," he said, looking straight at them.

Garotte made no reply, but walked straight on. Pomfrette stepped swiftly in front of the mealman. There was fury in his face—fury and danger; his hair was disordered, his eyes afire.

"Good-day, mealman," he said, and waited. "Duclosse," called Garotte warningly, "remember!" Duclosse's knees shook, and his face became mottled like a piece of soap; he pushed his fingers into his shirt and touched the Agnus Dei that he carried there. That and Garotte's words gave him courage. He scarcely knew what he said, but it had meaning. "Good-bye—leper," he answered.

Pomfrette's arm flew out to throw the pitcher at the mealman's head, but Duclosse, with a grunt of terror, flung up in front of his face the small bag of meal that he carried, the contents pouring over his waistcoat from a loose corner. The picture was so ludicrous that Pomfrette laughed with a devilish humour, and flinging the pitcher at the bag, he walked away towards his own house. Duclosse, pale and frightened, stepped from among the fragments of crockery, and with backward glances towards Pomfrette joined his comrade.

"Lime-burner," he said, sitting down on the bag of meal, and mechanically twisting tight the loose, leaking corner, "the devil's in that leper."

"He was a good enough fellow once," answered Garotte, watching Pomfrette.

"I drank with him at five o'clock yesterday," said Duclosse philosophically. "He was fit for any company then; now he's fit for none."

Garotte looked wise. "Mealman," said he, "it takes years to make folks love you; you can make them hate you in an hour. *La! La!* it's easier to hate than to love. Come along, m'sieu' dusty-belly."

Pomfrette's life in Pontiac went on as it began that day. Not once a day, and sometimes not once in twenty days, did any human being speak to him. The village baker would not sell him bread; his groceries he had to buy from the neighbouring parishes, for the grocer's flighty wife called for the constable when he entered the bake-shop of Pontiac. He had to bake his own bread, and do his own cooking, washing, cleaning, and gardening. His hair grew long and his clothes became shabbier. At last, when he needed a new suit—so torn had his others become at woodchopping and many kinds of work—he went to the village tailor, and was promptly told that nothing but Luc Pomfrette's grave-clothes would be cut and made in that house.

When he walked down to the Four Corners the street emptied at once, and the lonely man with the tinkling bell of honour at his knee felt the whole world falling away from sight and touch and sound of him. Once when he went into the Louis Quinze every man present stole away in silence, and the landlord himself, without a word, turned and left the bar. At that, with a hoarse laugh, Pomfrette poured out a glass of brandy, drank it off, and left a shilling on the counter. The next morning he found the shilling, wrapped in a piece of paper, just inside his door; it had been pushed underneath. On the paper was written: "It is cursed." Presently his dog died, and the day afterwards he suddenly disappeared from Pontiac, and wandered on to Ste. Gabrielle, Ribeaux, and Ville Bambord. But his shame had gone before him, and people shunned him everywhere, even the roughest. No one who knew him would shelter him. He slept in barns and in the woods until the winter came and snow lay thick upon the ground. Thin and haggard, and with nothing left of his old self but his deep brown eyes and curling hair, and his unhappy name and fame, he turned back again to Pontiac. His spirit was sullen and hard, his heart closed against repentance. Had not the Church and Pontiac and the world punished him beyond his deserts for a moment's madness brought on by a great shock!

II

One bright, sunshiny day of early winter, he trudged through the snow-banked street of Pontiac back to his home. Men he once knew well, and had worked with, passed him in a sled on their way to the great shanty in the backwoods. They halted in their singing for a moment when they saw him; then, turning their heads from him, dashed off, carolling lustily:

> "Ah, ah, Babette,
>   We go away;
> But we will come
>   Again, Babette,—
> Again back home,
>   On Easter Day,—
> Back home to play
>   On Easter Day,
> Babette! Babette!"

"Babette! Babette!" The words followed him, ringing in his ears long after the men had become a mere fading point in the white horizon behind him.

This was not the same world that he had known, not the same Pontiac. Suddenly he stopped short in the road.

"Curse them! Curse them! Curse them all!" he cried in a cracked, strange voice. A woman hurrying across the street heard him, and went the faster, shutting her ears. A little boy stood still and looked at him in wonder. Everything he saw maddened him. He turned sharp round and hurried to the Louis Quinze. Throwing open the door, he stepped inside. Half-a-dozen men were there with the landlord. When they saw him, they started, confused and dismayed. He stood still for a moment, looking at them with glowering brows.

"Good-day," he said. "How goes it?"

No one answered. A little apart from the others sat Medallion the auctioneer. He was a Protestant, and the curse on his baptism uttered by Pomfrette was not so heinous in his sight. For the other oath, it was another matter. Still, he was sorry for the man. In any case, it was not his cue to interfere; and Luc was being punished according to his bringing up and to the standards familiar to him. Medallion had never refused to speak to him, but he had done nothing more. There was no reason why he should provoke the enmity of the parish unnecessarily; and up to this point Pomfrette had shifted for himself after a fashion, if a hard fashion.

With a bitter laugh, Pomfrette turned to the little bar.

"Brandy," he said; "brandy, my Bourienne."

The landlord shrugged his shoulder, and looked the other way.

"Brandy," he repeated. Still there was no sign.

There was a wicked look in his face, from which the landlord shrank back—shrank so far that he carried himself among the others, and stood there, half frightened, half dumfounded.

Pomfrette pulled out a greasy dollar-bill from his pocket—the last he owned in the world—and threw it on the counter. Then he reached over, caught up a brandy-bottle from the shelf, knocked off the neck with a knife, and, pouring a tumblerful, drank it off at a gasp.

His head came up, his shoulders straightened out, his eyes snapped fire. He laughed aloud, a sardonic, wild, coarse laugh, and he shivered once or twice violently, in spite of the brandy he had drunk.

"You won't speak to me, eh? Won't you? Curse you! Pass me on the other side—so! Look at me. I am the worst man in the world, eh? Judas is nothing—no! Ack, what are you, to turn your back on me? Listen to me! You, there, Muroc, with your charcoal face, who was it walk thirty miles in the dead of winter to bring a doctor to your wife, eh? She die, but that is no matter—who was it? It was Luc Pomfrette. You, Alphonse Durien, who was it drag you out of the bog at the Cote Chaudière? It was Luc Pomfrette. You, Jacques Baby, who was it that lied for you to the Protestant girl at Faribeau? Just Luc Pomfrette. You two, Jean and Nicolas Mariban, who was it lent you a hunderd dollars when you lose all your money at cards? Ha, ha, ha! Only that beast Luc Pomfrette! Mother of Heaven, such a beast is he—eh, Limon Rouge?—such a beast that used to give your Victorine little silver things, and feed her with bread and sugar and buttermilk pop.[22] Ah, my dear Limon Rouge, how is it all different now!"

---

[22] A soup popular in the nineteenth century made with fermented milk, flour, and butter.

He raised the bottle and drank long from the ragged neck. When he took it away from his mouth not much more than half remained in the quart bottle. Blood was dripping upon his beard from a cut on his lip, and from there to the ground.

"And you, M'sieu' Bourienne," he cried hoarsely, "do I not remember that dear M'sieu' Bourienne, when he beg me to leave Pontiac for a little while that I not give evidence in court against him? *Eh bien!* you all walk by me now, as if I was the father of smallpox, and not Luc Pomfrette—only Luc Pomfrette, who spits at every one of you for a pack of cowards and hypocrites."

He thrust the bottle inside his coat, went to the door, flung it open with a bang, and strode out into the street, muttering as he went. As the landlord came to close the door Medallion said:

"The leper has a memory, my friends." Then he also walked out, and went to his office depressed, for the face of the man haunted him.

Pomfrette reached his deserted, cheerless house. There was not a stick of fire-wood in the shed, not a thing to eat or drink in cellar or cupboard. The door of the shed at the back was open, and the dog-chains lay covered with frost and half embedded in mud. With a shiver of misery Pomfrette raised the brandy to his mouth, drank every drop, and threw the bottle on the floor. Then he went to the front door, opened it, and stepped outside. His foot slipped, and he tumbled head forward into the snow. Once or twice he half raised himself, but fell back again, and presently lay still. The frost caught his ears and iced them; it began to creep over his cheeks; it made his fingers white, like a leper's.

He would soon have stiffened for ever had not Parpon the dwarf, passing along the road, seen the open door and the sprawling body, and come and drawn Pomfrette inside the house. He rubbed the face and hands and ears of the unconscious man with snow till the whiteness disappeared, and, taking off the boots, did the same with the toes; after which he drew the body to a piece of rag carpet beside the stove, threw some blankets over it, and, hurrying out, cut up some fence rails, and soon had a fire going in the stove.

Then he trotted out of the house and away to the Little Chemist, who came passively with him. All that day, and for many days, they fought to save Pomfrette's life. The Curé came also; but Pomfrette was in fever and delirium. Yet the good M. Fabre's presence, as it ever did, gave an air of calm and comfort to the place. Parpon's hands alone cared for the house; he did all that was to be done; no woman had entered the place since Pomfrette's cousin, old Mme. Burgoyne, left it on the day of his shame.

When at last Pomfrette opened his eyes, and saw the Curé standing beside him, he turned his face to the wall, and to the exhortation addressed to him he answered nothing. At last the Curé left him, and came no more; and he bade Parpon do the same as soon as Pomfrette was able to leave his bed.

But Parpon did as he willed. He had been in Pontiac only a few days since the painful business in front of the Louis Quinze. Where he had been and what doing no one asked, for he was mysterious in his movements, and always uncommunicative, and people did not care to tempt his inhospitable tongue. When Pomfrette was so far recovered that he might be left alone, Parpon said to him one evening:

"Pomfrette, you must go to Mass next Sunday."

"I said I wouldn't go till I was carried there, and I mean it—that's so," was the morose reply.

"What made you curse like that—so damnable?" asked Parpon furtively.

"That's my own business. It doesn't matter to anybody but me."

"And you said the Curé lied—the good M'sieu' Fabre—him like a saint."

"I said he lied, and I'd say it again, and tell the truth."

"But if you went to Mass, and took your penance, and—"

"Yes, I know; they'd forgive me, and I'd get absolution, and they'd all speak to me again, and it would be, 'Good-day, Luc,' and 'Very good, Luc,' and 'What a gay heart has Luc, the good fellow!' Ah, I know. They curse in the heart when the whole world go wrong for them; no one hears. I curse out loud. I'm not a hypocrite, and no one thinks me fit to live. Ack, what is the good!"

Parpon did not respond at once. At last, dropping his chin in his hand and his elbow on his knee, as he squatted on the table, he said:

"But if the girl got sorry—"

For a time there was no sound save the whirring of the fire in the stove and the hard breathing of the sick man. His eyes were staring hard at Parpon. At last he said, slowly and fiercely:

"What do you know?"

"What others might know if they had eyes and sense; but they haven't. What would you do if that Junie come back?"

"I would kill her." His look was murderous.

"Bah, you would kiss her first, just the same!"

"What of that? I would kiss her because—because there is no face like hers in the world; and I'd kill her for her bad heart."

"What did she do?" Pomfrette's hands clinched.

"What's in my own noddle, and not for anyone else," he answered sulkily.

'*Tiens, tiens,* what a close mouth! What did she do? Who knows? What you *think* she do, it's this. You think she pretends to love you, and you leave all your money with her. She is to buy masses for your father's soul; she is to pay money to the Curé for the good of the Church; she is to buy a little here, a little there, for the house you and she are going to live in, the wedding and the dancing over. Very well. Ah, my Pomfrette, what is the end you think? She run away with Dicey the Protestant, and take your money with her. Eh, is that so?"

For answer there came a sob, and then a terrible burst of weeping and anger and passionate denunciations—against Junie Gauloir, against Pontiac, against the world.

Parpon held his peace.

The days, weeks, and months went by; and the months stretched to three years.

In all that time Pomfrette came and went through Pontiac, shunned and unrepentant. His silent, gloomy endurance was almost an affront to Pontiac; and if the wiser ones, the Curé, the Avocat, the Little Chemist, and Medallion, were more sorry than offended, they stood aloof till the man should in some manner redeem himself, and repent of his horrid blasphemy. But one person persistently defied Church and people, Curé and voyageur. Parpon openly and boldly walked with Pomfrette, talked with him, and occasionally visited his house.

Luc made hard shifts to live. He grew everything that he ate, vegetables and grains. Parpon showed him how to make his own flour in primitive fashion, for no miller in any parish near would sell him flour, and he had no money to buy it, nor would anyone who knew him give him work. And after his return to Pontiac he never asked for it. His mood was defiant, morbid, stern. His wood he chopped from the common known as No-Man's Land. His clothes he made himself out of the skins of deer that he shot; when his powder and shot gave out, he killed the deer with bow and arrow.

III

The end came at last. Luc was taken ill. For four days, all alone, he lay burning with fever and inflammation, and when Parpon found him he was almost dead. Then began a fight for life again, in which Parpon was the only physician; for Pomfrette would not allow the Little Chemist or a doctor near him. Parpon at last gave up hope; but one night, when he came back from the village, he saw, to his joy, old Mme. Dégardy ("Crazy Joan" she was called) sitting by Pomfrette's bedside. He did not disturb her, for she had no love for him, and he waited till she had gone. When he came into the room again he found Pomfrette in a sweet sleep, and a jug of tincture, with a little tin cup, placed by the bed. Time and again he had sent for Mme. Dégardy, but she would not come. She had answered that the dear Luc could go to the devil for all of her; he'd find better company down below than in Pontiac.

But for a whim, perhaps, she had come at last without asking, and as a consequence Luc returned to the world, a mere bundle of bones.

It was still while he was only a bundle of bones that one Sunday morning, Parpon, without a word, lifted him up in his arms and carried him out of the house. Pomfrette did not speak at first: it seemed scarcely worthwhile; he was so weak he did not care.

"Where are you going?" he said at last, as they came well into the village. The bell in St. Saviour's had stopped ringing for Mass, and the streets were almost empty.

"I'm taking you to Mass," said Parpon, puffing under his load, for Pomfrette made an ungainly burden. "Hand of a little devil, no!" cried Pomfrette, startled. "I said I'd never go to Mass again, and I never will."

"You said you'd never go to Mass till you were carried; so it's all right."

Once or twice Pomfrette struggled, but Parpon held him tight, saying:

"It's no use; you must come; we've had enough. Besides—"

"Besides what?" asked Pomfrette faintly.

"Never mind," answered Parpon.

At a word from Parpon the shrivelled old sexton cleared a way through the aisle, making a stir, through which the silver bell at Pomfrette's knee tinkled, in answer, as it were, to the tinkling of the acolyte's bell in the sanctuary.[23] People turned at the sound, women stopped telling their beads, some of the choir forgot their chanting. A strange feeling passed through the church, and reached and startled the Curé as he recited the Mass. He turned round and saw Parpon laying Pomfrette down at the chancel steps.[24] His voice shook a little as he intoned the ritual, and as he raised the sacred elements tears rolled down his cheeks.

---

[23] The ringing of sanctuary bells is an 800-year-old tradition of the Catholic Mass; usually these are small hand-held bells rung as communion is about to be taken. An acolyte is a cleric who performs certain offices including ringing of the sanctuary bells. It is a counterpoint to the bell that Pomfrette wears on his leg.

[24] The chancel is the part of a church containing the altar, sanctuary, and choir. In other words, Paron lays Luc Pomfrette at the base of the steps leading up to the altar.

From a distant corner of the gallery a deeply veiled woman also looked down at Pomfrette, and her hand trembled on the desk before her.

At last the Curé came forward to the chancel steps.

"What is it, Parpon?" he asked gravely.

"It is Luc Pomfrette, M'sieu' le Curé." Pomfrette's eyes were closed.

"He swore that he would never come to Mass again," answered the good priest.

"Till he was carried, M'sieu' le Curé—and I've carried him."

"Did you come of your own free will, and with a repentant heart, Luc Pomfrette?" asked the Curé.

"I did not know I was coming—no." Pomfrette's brown eyes met the priest's unflinchingly.

"You have defied God, and yet He has spared your life."

"I'd rather have died," answered the sick man simply.

"Died, and been cast to perdition!"

"I'm used to that; I've had a bad time here in Pontiac."

His thin hands moved restlessly. His leg moved, and the little bell tinkled—the bell that had been like the bell of a leper these years past.

"But you live, and you have years yet before you, in the providence of God. Luc Pomfrette, you blasphemed against your baptism, and horribly against God himself. Luc"—his voice got softer—"I knew your mother, and she was almost too weak to hold you when you were baptised, for you made a great to-do about coming into the world. She had a face like a saint—so sweet, so patient. You were her only child, and your baptism was more to her than her marriage even, or any other thing in this world. The day after your baptism she died. What do you think were her last words?"

There was a hectic flush on Pomfrette's face, and his eyes were intense and burning as they looked up fixedly at the Curé.

"I can't think any more," answered Pomfrette slowly. "I've no head."

"What she said is for your heart, not for your head, Luc," rejoined the Curé gently. "She wandered in her mind, and at the last she raised herself up in her bed, and lifting her finger like this"—he made the gesture of benediction—"she said, 'Luc Michée, I baptise you in the name of the Father, and of the Son, and of the Holy Ghost. Amen.' Then she whispered softly: 'God bless my dear Luc Michée! Holy Mother pray for him!' These were her last words, and I took you from her arms. What have you to say, Luc Michée?"

The woman in the gallery was weeping silently behind her thick veil, and her worn hand clutched the desk in front of her convulsively. Presently she arose and made her way down the stair, almost unnoticed. Two or three times Luc tried to speak, but could not. "Lift me up," he said brokenly, at last.

Parpon and the Little Chemist raised him to his feet, and held him, his shaking hands resting on their shoulders, his lank body tottering above and between them.

Looking at the congregation, he said slowly: "I'll suffer till I die for cursing my baptism, and God will twist my neck in purgatory for—"

"Luc," the Curé interrupted, "say that you repent."

"I'm sorry, and I ask you all to forgive me, and I'll confess to the Curé, and take my penance, and—" he paused, for breathing hurt him.

At that moment the woman in black who had been in the gallery came quickly forward. Parpon saw her, frowned, and waved her back; but she came on. At the chancel steps she raised her veil, and a murmur of recognition and wonder ran through the church. Pomfrette's face was pitiful to see—drawn, staring.

"Junie!" he said hoarsely.

Her eyes were red with weeping, her face was very pale. "M'sieu' le Curé," she said, "you must listen to me"—the Curé's face had become forbidding—"sinner though I am. You want to be just, don't you? Ah, listen! I was to be married to Luc Pomfrette, but I did not love him—then. He had loved me for years, and his father and my father wished it—as you know, M'sieu' le Curé. So after a while I said I would; but I begged him that he wouldn't say anything about it till he come back from his next journey on the river. I did not love him enough—then. He left all his money with me: some to pay for Masses for his father's soul, some to buy things for—for our home; and the rest to keep till he came back."

"Yes, yes," said Pomfrette, his eyes fixed painfully on her face—"yes, yes."

"The day after Luc went away John Dicey the Protestant come to me. I'd always liked him; he could talk as Luc couldn't, and it sounded nice. I listened and listened. He knew about Luc and about the money and all. Then he talked to me. I was all wild in the head, and things went round and round, and oh, how I hated to marry Luc—then! So after he had talked a long while I said yes, I would go with him and marry him—a Protestant—for I loved him. I don't know why or how."

Pomfrette trembled so that Parpon and the Little Chemist made him sit down, and he leaned against their shoulders, while Junie went on:

"I gave him Luc's money to go and give to Parpon here, for I was too ashamed to go myself. And I wrote a little note to Luc, and sent it with the money. I believed in John Dicey, of course. He came back, and said that he had seen Parpon and had done it all right; then we went away to Montreal and got married. The very first day at Montreal, I found out that he had Luc's money. It was awful. I went mad, and he got angry and left me alone, and didn't come back. A week afterwards he was killed, and I didn't know it for a long time. But I began to work, for I wanted to pay back Luc's money. It was very slow, and I worked hard. Will it never be finished, I say. At last Parpon find me, and I tell him all—all except that John Dicey was dead; and I did not know that. I made him promise to tell nobody; but he knows all about my life since then. Then I find out one day that John Dicey is dead, and I get from the gover'ment a hundred dollars of the money he stole. It was found on him when he was killed. I work for six months longer, and now I come back—with Luc's money."

She drew from her pocket a packet of notes, and put it in Luc's hands. He took it dazedly, then dropped it, and the Little Chemist picked it up; he had no prescription like that in his pharmacopoeia.

"That's how I've lived," she said, and she handed a letter to the Curé.

It was from a priest in Montreal, setting forth the history of her career in that city, her repentance for her elopement and the sin of marrying a Protestant, and her good life. She had wished to do her penance in Pontiac, and it remained to M'sieu' le Curé to set it.

The Curé's face relaxed, and a rare gentleness came into it.

He read the letter aloud. Luc once more struggled to his feet, eagerly listening.

"You did not love Luc?" the Curé asked Junie, meaningly.

"I did not love Luc—then," she answered, a flush going over her face.

"You loved Junie?" the Curé said to Pomfrette. "I could have killed her, but I've always loved her," answered Luc. Then he raised his voice excitedly: "I love her, love her, love her—but what's the good! She'd never've been happy with me. Look what my love drove her to! What's the good, at all!"

"She said she did not love you *then*, Luc Michée," said Parpon, interrupting. "Luc Michée, you're a fool as well as a sinner. Speak up, Junie."

"I used to tell him that I didn't love him; I only liked him. I was honest. Well, I am honest still. I love him now."

A sound of joy broke from Luc's lips, and he stretched out his arms to her, but the Curé; stopped that. "Not here," he said. "Your sins must first be considered. For penance—" He paused, looking at the two sad yet happy beings before him. The deep knowledge of life that was in him impelled him to continue gently:

"For penance you shall bear the remembrance of each other's sins. And now to God the Father—"

He turned towards the altar, and raised his hands in the ascription.

As he knelt to pray before he entered the pulpit, he heard the tinkling of the little bell of honour at the knee of Luc, as Junie and Parpon helped him from the church.

A SON OF THE
WILDERNESS

Rachette told the story to Medallion and the Little Chemist's wife on Sunday after Mass, and because he was vain of his English he forsook his own tongue and paid tribute to the Anglo-Saxon.

"Ah, she was so purty, that Norinne, when she drive through the parishes all twelve days, after the wedding, a dance every night, and her eyes and cheeks on fire all the time. And Bargon, bagosh! that Bargon, he have a pair of shoulders like a wall, and five hunder' dollars and a horse and wagon. Bagosh, I say that time: 'Bargon he have put a belt round the world and buckle it tight to him—all right, ver' good.' I say to him: 'Bargon, what you do when you get ver' rich out on the Souris River in the prairie west?' He laugh and throw up his hands, for he have not many words any kind. And the dam little dwarf Parpon, he say: 'He will have flowers on the table and ice on the butter, and a wheel in his head.'

119

"And Bargon laugh and say: 'I will have plenty for my friends to eat and drink and a ver' fine time.'

" 'Good,' we all say—'Bagosh!' So they make the trip through twelve parish, and the fiddles go all the time, and I am what you say 'best man' with Bargon. I go all the time, and Lucette Dargois, she go with me and her brother—holy, what an eye had she in her head, that Lucette! As we go we sing a song all right, and there is no one sing so better as Norinne:

> "'C'est la belle Françoise,
> Allons gai!
> C'est la belle Françoise,
> Qui veut se marier,
> Ma luron lurette!
> Qui veut se marier,
> Ma luron lure!'

"Ver' good, bagosh! Norinne and Bargon they go out to the Souris, and Bargon have a hunder' acre, and he put up a house and a shed not ver' big, and he carry his head high and his shoulders like a wall; yes, yes. First year it is pretty good time, and Norinne's cheeks—ah, like an apple they. Bimeby[25] a baby laugh up at Bargon from Norinne's lap. I am on the Souris at a saw-mill then, and on Sunday sometime I go up to see Bargon and Norinne. I t'ink that baby is so dam funny; I laugh and pinch his nose. His name is Marie, and I say I marry him pretty quick someday. We have plenty hot cake, and beans and pork, and a little how-you-are from a jar behin' the door.

[25] By and by.

"Next year it is not so good. There is a bad crop and hard time, and Bargon he owe two hunder' dollar, and he pay int'rest. Norinne, she do all the work, and that little Marie, there is dam funny in him, and Norinne, she keep go, go, all the time, early and late, and she get ver' thin and quiet. So I go up from the mill more times, and I bring fol-lols[26] for that Marie, for you know I said I go to marry him some day. And when I see how Bargon shoulders stoop and his eye get dull, and there is nothing in the jar behin' the door, I fetch a horn with me, and my fiddle, and, bagosh! there is happy sit-you-down. I make Bargon sing 'La Belle Françoise,' and then just before I go I make them laugh, for I stand by the cradle and I sing to that Marie:

> "'Adieu, belle Françoise;
> Allons gai!
> Adieu, belle Françoise!
> Moi, je te marierai,
> Ma luron lurette! Moi,
> je te marierai,
> Ma luron lure!'

"So; and another year it go along, and Bargon he know that if there come bad crop it is good-bye-my lover with himselves. He owe two hunder' and fifty dollar. It is the spring at Easter, and I go up to him and Norinne, for there is no Mass, and Pontiac is too far away off. We stan' at the door and look out, and all the prairie is green, and the sun stan' up high like a light on a pole, and the birds fly by ver' busy looking for the summer and the prairie-flower.

---

[26] Trinkets, ornaments associated with female dress.

"'Bargon,' I say—and I give him a horn of old rye—'here's to le bon Dieu!'

"'Le bon Dieu, and a good harvest!' he say.

"I hear someone give a long breath behin', and I look round; but, no, it is Norinne with a smile—for she never grumble—bagosh! What purty eyes she have in her head! She have that Marie in her arms, and I say to Bargon it is like the Madonne in the Notre Dame at Montreal. He nod his head. 'C'est le bon Dieu—it is the good God,' he say.

"Before I go I take a piece of palm[27]—it come from the Notre Dame; it is all bless by the Pope—and I nail it to the door of the house. 'For luck,' I say. Then I laugh, and I speak out to the prairie: 'Come along, good summer; come along, good crop; come two hunder' and fifty dollars for Gal Bargon.' Ver' quiet I give Norinne twenty dollar, but she will not take him. 'For Marie,' then I say: 'I go to marry him, bimeby.' But she say: 'Keep it and give it to Marie yourself someday.'

"She smile at me, then she have a little tear in her eye, and she nod to where Bargon stare' houtside, and she say: 'If this summer go wrong, it will kill him. He work and work and fret and worry for me and Marie, and sometimes he just sit and look at me and say not a word.'

"I say to her that there will be good crop, and next year we will be ver' happy. So, the time go on, and I send up a leetla snack of pork and molass' and tabac, and sugar and tea, and I get a letter from Bargon bimeby, and he say that heverything go right, he t'ink, this

---

[27] A blessed piece of palm leaf; the palm tree has an important association with Chris in Catholicism.

summer. He say I must come up. It is not dam easy to go in the summer, when the mill run night and day; but I say I will go.

"When I get up to Bargon's I laugh, for all the hunder' acre is ver' fine, and Bargon stan' hin the door, and stretch out his hand, and say: 'Rachette, there is six hunder' dollar for me.' I nod my head, and fetch out a horn, and he have one, his eyes all bright like a lime-kiln. He is thin and square, and his beard grow ver' thick and rough and long, and his hands are like planks. Norinne, she is ver' happy, too, and Marie bite on my finger, and I give him sugar-stick to suck.

"Bimeby Norinne say to me, ver' soft: 'If a hailstorm or a hot wind come, that is the end of it all, and of my poor Gal.'

"What I do? I laugh and ketch Marie under the arms, and I sit down, and I put him on my foot, and I sing that dam funny English song—'Here We Go to Banbury Cross.' An' I say: 'It will be all as happy as Marie pretty quick. Bargon he will have six hunder' dollar, and you a new dress and a hired girl to help you.'

"But all the time that day I think about a hail-storm or a hot wind whenever I look out on that hunder' acre farm. It is so beautiful, as you can guess—the wheat, the barley, the corn, the potatoes, the turnip, all green like sea-water, and pigeons and wild ducks flying up and down, and the horse and the ox standing in a field ver' comfer'ble.

"We have good time that day, and go to bed all happy that night. I get up at five o'clock, an' I go hout. Bargon stan' there looking hout on his field with the horse-bridle in his hand. 'The air not feel right,' he say to me. I t'ink the same, but I say to him: 'Your head not feel right—him too sof'.' He shake his head and go down to the field for his horse and ox, and hitch them up together, and go to work making a road.

"It is about ten o'clock when the dam thing come. Piff! go a hot splash of air in my face, and then I know that it is all up with Gal Bargon. A month after it is no matter, for the grain is ripe then, but now, when it is green, it is sure death to it all. I turn sick in my stomich, and I turn round and see Norinne stan' hin the door, all white, and she make her hand go as that, like she push back that hot wind.

"'Where is Gal?' she say. 'I must go to him.' 'No,' I say, 'I will fetch him. You stay with Marie.' Then I go ver' quick for Gal, and I find him, his hands all shut like that! and he shake them at the sky, and he say not a word, but his face, it go wild, and his eyes spin round in his head. I put my hand on his arm and say: 'Come home, Gal. Come home, and speak kind to Norinne and Marie.'

"I can see that hot wind lean down and twist the grain about—a dam devil thing from the Arzone desert down South. I take Gal back home, and we sit there all day, and all the nex' day, and a leetla more, and when we have look enough, there is no grain on that hunder' acre farm—only a dry-up prairie, all grey and limp. My skin is bake and rough, but when I look at Gal Bargon I know that his heart is dry like a bone, and, as Parpon say that back time, he have a wheel in his head. Norinne she is quiet, and she sit with her hand on his shoulder, and give him Marie to hold.

"But it is no good; it is all over. So I say: 'Let us go back to Pontiac. What is the good for to be rich? Let us be poor and happy once more.'

"And Norinne she look glad, and get up and say: 'Yes, let us go back.' But all at once she sit down with Marie in her arms, and cry—bagosh, I never see a woman cry like that!

"So we start back for Pontiac with the horse and the ox and some pork and bread and molass'. But Gal Bargon never hold up his head, but go silent, silent, and he not sleep at night. One night he walk away on the prairie, and when he come back he have a great pain. So he lie down, and we sit by him, an' he die. But once he whisper to me, and Norinne not hear: 'You say you will marry him, Rachette?' and I say, 'I will.'

"'C'est le bon Dieu!' he say at the last, but he say it with a little laugh. I think he have a wheel in his head. But bimeby, yiste'day, Norinne and Marie and I come to Pontiac."

The Little Chemist's wife dried her eyes, and Medallion said in French: "Poor Norinne! Poor Norinne! And so, Rachette, you are going to marry Marie, by-and-bye?" There was a quizzical look in Medallion's eyes.

Rachette threw up his chin a little. "I'm going to marry Norinne on New Year's Day," he said.

"Bagosh, poor Norinne!" said Medallion, in a queer sort of tone. "It is the way of the world," he added. "I'll wait for Marie myself."

It looks as if he meant to, for she has no better friend. He talks to her much of Gal Bargon; of which her mother is glad.

A WORKER IN STONE

At the beginning he was only a tombstone-cutter. His name was François Lagarre. He was but twenty years old when he stepped into the shop where the old tombstone-cutter had worked for forty years. Picking up the hammer and chisel which the old man had dropped when he fell dead at the end of a long hot day's labour, he finished the half-carved tombstone, and gave the price of it to the widow. Then, going to the Seigneur and Curé, he asked them to buy the shop and tools for him, and let him pay rent until he could take the place off their hands.

They did as he asked, and in two years he had bought and paid for the place, and had a few dollars to the good. During one of the two years a small-pox epidemic passed over Pontiac, and he was busy night and day. It was during this time that some good Catholics came to him with an heretical Protestant suggestion to carve a couplet or verse of poetry on the tombstones they ordered. They themselves, in most cases, knew none, and they asked François to supply them—as though he kept them in stock like marble and sand-

126

paper. He had no collection of suitable epitaphs, and, besides, he did not know whether it was right to use them. Like all his race in New France he was jealous of any inroads of Protestantism, or what the Little Chemist called "Englishness." The good M. Fabre, the Curé, saw no harm in it, but said he could not speak for any one's grief. What the bereaved folk felt they themselves must put in words upon the stone. But still François might bring all the epitaphs to him before they were carved, and he would approve or disapprove, correct or reject, as the case might be.

At first he rejected many, for they were mostly conventional couplets, taken unknowingly from Protestant sources by mourning Catholics. But presently all that was changed, and the Curé one day had laid before him three epitaphs, each of which left his hand unrevised and untouched; and when he passed them back to François his eyes were moist, for he was a man truly after God's own heart, and full of humanity.

"Will you read them to me, François?" he said, as the worker in stone was about to put the paper back in his pocket. "Give the names of the dead at the same time."

So François read:

"Gustave Narrois, aged seventy-two years—"

"Yes, yes," interrupted the Curé, "the unhappy yet happy Gustave, hung by the English, and cut down just in time to save him—an innocent man. For thirty years my sexton. God rest his soul! Well now, the epitaph."

François read it:

"Poor as a sparrow was I,
Yet I was saved like a king;

> I heard the death-bells ring,
>
> Yet I saw a light in the sky:
>
> And now to my Father I wing."

The Curé nodded his head. "Go on; the next," he said.

"Annette John, aged twenty years—"

"So. The daughter of Chief John. When Queen Anne of England[28] was on the throne she sent Chief John's grandfather a gold cup and a hundred pounds. The girl loved, but would not marry, that she might keep Chief John from drinking. A saint, François! What have they said of her?"

François smoothed out the paper and read:

> "A little while I saw the world go by
>
> A little doorway that I called my own,
>
> A loaf, a cup of water, and a bed had I,
>
> A shrine of Jesus, where I knelt alone:
>
> And now alone I bid the world good-bye."

The Curé turned his head away. "Go on," he said sadly. "Chief John has lost his right hand. Go on."

"Henri Rouget."

"Aged thirty years," again interrupted the Curé. "Henri Rouget, idiot; as young as the morning. For man grows old only by what he suffers, and what he forgives, and what he sins. What have you to say for Henri Rouget, my François?"

And François read:

---

[28] Anne (1665–1714) became Queen of England, Scotland, and Ireland in 1702. In 1707, England and Scotland were united as the single kingdom of Great Britain, and so Anne became the first monarch of Great Britain.

"I was a fool; nothing had I to know
Of men, and naught to men had I to give.
God gave me nothing; now to God I go,
Now ask for pain, for bread,
Life for my brain: dead,
By God's love I shall then begin to live."

The priest rose to his feet and put a hand on the young man's shoulder.

"Do you know, François," he said, half sadly, "do you know, you have the true thing in you. Come often to me, my son, and bring all these things—all you write."

While the Curé troubled himself about his future, François began to work upon a monument for the grave of a dozen soldiers of Pontiac who were killed in the War of the Patriots.[29] They had died for a mistaken cause, and had been buried on the field of battle. Long ago something would have been done to commemorate them but that three of them were Protestants, and difficulties had been raised by the bigoted. But François thought only of the young men in their common grave at St. Eustache. He remembered when they went away one bright morning, full of the joy of an erring patriotism, of the ardour of a weak but fascinating cause: race against race, the conquered against the conquerors, the usurped against the usurpers.

In the space before the parish church it stands—a broken shaft, with an unwound wreath straying down its sides; a monument of

[29] The 1837 armed conflict between the rebels of Quebec, then Lower Canada, and the British colonial government over a range of economic and perceived racial grievances. Casualties on the rebel side were 73 dead, 1,600 injured or captured, and 28 executed for treason.

fine proportions, a white figure of beaten valour and erring ardour of youth and beautiful bad ambition. One Saturday night it was not there, and when next morning the people came to Mass it was there. All night had François and his men worked, and the first rays of the morning sun fell on the tall shivered shaft set firmly in its place. François was a happy man. All else that he had done had been wholly after a crude, staring convention, after rule and measure—an artisan's, a tombstone-cutter's labour. This was the work of a man with the heart and mind of an artist. When the people came to Mass they gazed and gazed, and now and then the weeping of a woman was heard, for among them were those whose sons and brothers were made memorable by this stone.

That day at the close of his sermon the Curé spoke of it, and said at the last: "That white shaft, dear brethren, is for us a sign of remembrance and a warning to our souls. In the name of race and for their love they sinned. But yet they sinned; and this monument, the gift and work of one young like them, ardent and desiring like them, is forever in our eyes the crucifixion of our wrong ambitions and our selfish aims.

"Nay, let us be wise and let us be good. They who rule us speak with foreign tongue, but their hearts desire our peace and a mutual regard. Pray that this be. And pray for the young and the daring and the foolish. And pray also that he who has given us here a good gift may find his thanks in our better-ordered lives, and that he may consecrate his parts and talents to the redeeming actions of this world."

And so began the awakening of François Lagarre; and so began his ambition and his peril.

For, as he passed from the church, the Seigneur touched him on the shoulder and introduced him to his English grandniece, come on a visit for the summer, the daughter of a London baronet. She had but just arrived, and she was feeling that first homesickness which succeeds transplanting. The face of the young worker in stone interested her; the idea of it all was romantic; the possibilities of the young man's life opened out before her. Why should not she give him his real start, win his gratitude, help him to his fame, and then, when it was won, be pointed out as a discoverer and a patron?

All these things flashed through her mind as they were introduced. The young man did not read the look in her eyes, but there was one other person in the crowd about the church steps who did read it, whose heart beat furiously, whose foot tapped the ground angrily—a black-haired, brown-eyed farmer's daughter, who instantly hated the yellow hair and rosy and golden face of the blue-eyed London lady; who could, that instant, have torn the silk gown from her graceful figure.

She was not disturbed without reason. And for the moment, even when she heard impertinent and incredulous fellows pooh-poohing the monument, and sharpening their rather dull wits upon its corners, she did not open her lips, when otherwise she would have spoken her mind with a vengeance; for Jeanne Marchand had a reputation for spirit and temper, and she spared no one when her blood was up. She had a touch of the vixen—an impetuous, loving, forceful mademoiselle, in marked contrast to the rather ascetic François, whose ways were more refined than his origin might seem to warrant.

'*Sapré,*' said Duclosse the mealman of the monument; "it's like a timber of cheese stuck up. What's that to make a fuss about?"

"Fig of Eden," muttered Jules Marmotte, with one eye on Jeanne, "any fool could saw a better-looking thing out of ice!"

"Pish," said fat Caroche the butcher, "that François has a rattle in his *capote*.[30] He'd spend his time better chipping bones on my meat-block."

But Jeanne could not bear this—the greasy whopping butcher-man!

"What, what, the messy stupid Caroche, who can't write his name," she said in a fury; "the sausage-potted Caroche, who doesn't remember that François Lagarre made his brother's tombstone, and charged him nothing for the verses he wrote for it, nor for the Agnus Dei he carved on it! No, Caroche does not remember his brother Ba'tiste the fighter, as brave as Caroche is a coward! He doesn't remember the verse on Ba'tiste's tombstone, does he?"

François heard this speech, and his eyes lighted tenderly as he looked at Jeanne: he loved this fury of defence and championship. Someone in the crowd turned to him and asked him to say the verses. At first he would not; but when Caroche said that it was only his fun, that he meant nothing against François, the young man recited the words slowly—an epitaph on one who was little better than a prize-fighter, a splendid bully.

Leaning a hand against the white shaft of the Patriot's Memory, he said:

> "Blows I have struck, and blows a-many taken,
> Wrestling I've fallen, and I've rose up again;
> Mostly I've stood—
> I've had good bone and blood;

---

[30] Hood.

Others went down, though fighting might and main.

Now death steps in—

Death the price of sin.

The fall it will be his; and though I strive and strain,

One blow will close my eyes, and I shall never waken."

"Good enough for Ba'tiste," said Duclosse the mealman.

The wave of feeling was now altogether with François, and presently he walked away with Jeanne Marchand and her mother, and the crowd dispersed. Jeanne was very happy for a few hours, but in the evening she was unhappy, for she saw François going towards the house of the Seigneur; and during many weeks she was still more unhappy, for every three or four days she saw the same thing.

Meanwhile François worked as he had never before worked in his life. Night and day he was shut in his shop, and for two months he came with no epitaphs for the Curé, and no new tombstones were set up in the graveyard. The influence of the lady at the Seigneury was upon him, and he himself believed it was for his salvation. She had told him of great pieces of sculpture she had seen, had sent and got from Quebec City, where he had never been, pictures of some of the world's masterpieces in sculpture, and he had lost himself in the study of them and in the depths of the girl's eyes. She meant no harm; the man interested her beyond what was reasonable in one of his station in life. That was all, and all there ever was.

Presently people began to gossip, and a story crept round that, in a new shed which he had built behind his shop, François was chiselling out of stone the nude figure of a woman. There were one or two who professed they had seen it. The wildest gossip said that the figure was that of the young lady at the Seigneury. François saw no more of Jeanne Marchand; he thought of her sometimes, but that was all. A fever of work was on him. Twice she came to the shed where he laboured, and knocked at the door. The first time, he asked who was there. When she told him he opened the door just a little way, smiled at her, caught her hand and pressed it, and, when she would have entered, said: "No, no, another day, Jeanne," and shut the door in her face.

She almost hated him because he had looked so happy. Still another day she came knocking. She called to him, and this time he opened the door and admitted her. That very hour she had heard again the story of the nude stone woman in the shed, and her heart was full of jealousy, fury, and suspicion. He was very quiet, he seemed tired. She did not notice that. Her heart had throbbed wildly as she stepped inside the shed. She looked round, all delirious eagerness for the nude figure.

There it was, covered up with a great canvas! Yes, there were the outlines of the figure. How shapely it seemed, even inside the canvas!

She stepped forward without a word, and snatched at the covering. He swiftly interposed and stopped her hand.

"I will see it," she said.

"Not to-day," he answered.

"I tell you I will." She wrenched her hand free and caught at the canvas. A naked foot and ankle showed. He pinioned her wrists with one hand and drew her towards the door, determination and anger in his face.

"You beast, you liar!" she said. "You beast! beast! beast!"

Then, with a burst of angry laughter, she opened the door herself. "You ain't fit to know," she said; "they told the truth about you. Now you can take the canvas off her. Good-bye!" With that she was gone.

The following day was Sunday. François did not attend Mass, and such strange scandalous reports had reached the Curé that he was both disturbed and indignant. That afternoon, after vespers (which François did not attend), the Curé made his way to the sculptor's workshop, followed by a number of parishioners.

The crowd increased, and when the Curé knocked at the door it seemed as if half the village was there.

The chief witness against François had been Jeanne Marchand. That very afternoon she had told the Curé, with indignation and bitterness, that there was no doubt about it; all that had been said was true.

François, with wonder and some confusion, admitted the Curé. When M. Fabre demanded that he be taken to the new workshop, François led the way. The crowd pushed after, and presently the place was full. A hundred eyes were fastened upon the canvas-covered statue, which had been the means of the young man's undoing.

Terrible things had been said—terrible things of François, and of the girl at the Seigneury. They knew the girl for a Protestant and an Englishwoman, and that in itself was a sort of sin. And now every ear was alert to hear what the Curé should say, what denunciation should come from his lips when the covering was removed. For that it should be removed was the determination of every man present. Virtue was at its supreme height in Pontiac that day. Lajeunesse the blacksmith, Muroc the charcoal-man, and twenty others were as intent upon preserving a high standard of morality, by force of arms, as if another Tarquin[31] were harbouring shame and crime in this cedar shed.

The whole thing came home to François with a choking, smothering force. Art, now in its very birth in his heart and life, was to be garroted. He had been unconscious of all the wicked things said about him: now he knew all!

"Remove the canvas from the figure," said the Curé sternly. Stubbornness and resentment filled François's breast. He did not stir.

"Do you oppose the command of the Church?" said the Curé, still more severely. "Remove the canvas."

"It is my work—my own: my idea, my stone, and the labour of my hands," said François doggedly.

The Curé turned to Lajeunesse and made a motion towards the statue. Lajeunesse, with a burning righteous joy, snatched off the canvas. There was one instant of confusion in the faces of all—of absolute silence. Then the crowd gasped. The Curé's hat came off, and every other hat followed. The Curé made the sign of the cross upon his breast and forehead, and every other man, woman, and child present did the same. Then all knelt, save François and the Curé himself.

What they saw was a statue of Christ, a beautiful benign figure; barefooted, with a girdle about his waist: the very truth and semblance of a man. The type was strong and yet delicate; vigorous and yet refined; crude and yet noble; a leader of men—the God-man, not the man-God.

---

[31] By tradition the last king of Rome, who established a reign of terror. After Tarquin's son raped the noblewoman Lucretia, revolt ensued and Tarquin was deposed.

After a moment's silence the Curé spoke. "François, my son," said he, "we have erred. 'All we like sheep have gone astray; we have followed each after his own way, but God hath laid on Him'—he looked towards the statue—'the iniquity of us all.'"

François stood still a moment gazing at the Curé, doggedly, bitterly; then he turned and looked scornfully at the crowd, now risen to their feet again. Among them was a girl crying as if her heart would break. It was Jeanne Marchand. He regarded her coldly.

"You were so ready to suspect," he said.

Then he turned once more to the Curé. "I meant it as my gift to the Church, monsieur le Curé—to Pontiac, where I was born again. I waked up here to what I might do in sculpture, and you—you all were so ready to suspect! Take it, it is my last gift."

He went to the statue, touched the hands of it lovingly, and stooped and kissed the feet. Then, without more words, he turned and left the shed and the house.

Pouring out into the street the people watched him cross the bridge that led into another parish—and into another world: for from that hour François Lagarre was never seen in Pontiac.

The statue that he made stands upon a little hill above the valley where the beaters of flax come in the autumn, through which the woodsmen pass in winter and in spring. But François Lagarre, under another name, works in another land.

While the Curé lived he heard of him and of his fame now and then, and to the day of his death he always prayed for him. He was wont to say to the little Avocat whenever François's name was mentioned:

'The spirit of a man will support him, but a wounded spirit who can bear?"

THE TRAGIC
COMEDY OF
ANNETTE

The chest of drawers, the bed, the bedding, the pieces of linen, and the pile of yarn had been ready for many months. Annette had made inventory of them every day since the *dot*[32] was complete—at first with a great deal of pride, after a time more shyly and wistfully: Bénoît did not come. He had said he would be down with the first drive of logs in the summer, and at the little church of St. Saviour's they would settle everything and get the Curé's blessing. Almost anybody would have believed in Bénoît. He had the brightest scarf, the merriest laugh, the quickest eyes, and the blackest head in Pontiac; and no one among the river drivers could sing like him. That was, he said gaily, because his earrings were gold, and not brass like those of his comrades. Thus Bénoît was a little vain, and

[32] Dowry.

something more; but old ladies such as the Little Chemist's wife said he was *galant*. Probably only Medallion the auctioneer and the Curé did not lose themselves in the general admiration; they thought he was to Annette like a farthing dip[33] to a holy candle.

Annette was the youngest of twelve, and one of a family of thirty—for some of her married brothers and sisters and their children lived in her father's long white house by the river. When Bénoît failed to come in the spring, they showed their pity for her by abusing him; and when she pleaded for him they said things which had an edge. They ended by offering to marry her to Farette, the old miller, to whom they owed money for flour. They brought Farette to the house at last, and she was patient while he ogled her, and smoked his strong *tabac*, and tried to sing. She was kind to him, and said nothing until, one day, urged by her brother Solime, he mumbled the childish chanson Bénoît sang the day he left, as he passed their house going up the river:

"High in a nest of the tam'rac tree,
    Swing under, so free, and swing over;
Swing under the sun and swing over the world,
    My snow-bird, my gay little lover
        My gay little lover, *don, don!... don, don!*

"When the winter is done I will come back home,
    To the nest swinging under and over,
Swinging under and over and waiting for me,
    Your rover, my snow-bird, your rover—
        Your lover and rover, *don, don!... don, don!*"

---

[33] A piece of bread dipped in hot fat and sold by pork butchers; compared to a "holy candle" the term suggests low status.

It was all very well in the mouth of the sprightly, sentimental Bénoît; it was hateful foolishness in Farette. Annette now came to her feet suddenly, her pale face showing defiance, and her big brown eyes flicking anger. She walked up to the miller and said: "You are old and ugly and a fool. But I do not hate you; I hate Solime, my brother, for bringing you here. There is the bill for the flour? Well, I will pay it myself—and you can go as soon as you like!"

Then she put on her coat and *capote* and mittens, and went to the door. "Where are you going, Ma'm'selle?" cried Solime, in high rage.

"I am going to M'sieu' Medallion," she said.

Hard profane words followed her, but she ran, and never stopped till she came to Medallion's house. He was not there. She found him at the Little Chemist's.

That night a pony and cart took away from the house of Annette's father the chest of drawers, the bed, the bedding, the pieces of linen, and the pile of yarn which had been made ready so long against Bénoît's coming. Medallion had said he could sell them at once, and he gave her the money that night; but this was after he had had a talk with the Curé, to whom Annette had told all. Medallion said he had been able to sell the things at once; but he did not tell her that they were stored in a loft of the Little Chemist's house, and that the Little Chemist's wife had wept over them and carried the case to the shrine of the Blessed Virgin.

It did not matter that the father and brothers stormed. Annette was firm; the *dot* was hers, and she would do as she wished. She carried the money to the miller. He took it grimly and gave her a receipt, grossly mis-spelled, and, as she was about to go, brought his fist heavily down on his leg and said: "*Mon Dieu*, it is brave—it is grand—it is an angel." Then he chuckled: "So, so! It was true. I am old, ugly, and a fool. Eh, well, I have my money!" Then he took to counting it over in his hand, forgetting her, and she left him growling gleefully over it.

She had not a happy life, but her people left her alone, for the Curé had said stern things to them. All during the winter she went out fishing every day at a great hole in the ice—bitter cold work, and fit only for a man; but she caught many fish, and little by little laid aside pennies to buy things to replace what she had sold. It had been a hard trial to her to sell them. But for the kind-hearted Curé she would have repined. The worst thing happened, however, when the ring Bénoît had given her dropped from her thin finger into the water where she was fishing. Then a shadow descended on her, and she grew almost unearthly in the anxious patience of her face. The Little Chemist's wife declared that the look was death. Perhaps it would have been if Medallion had not sent a lad down to the bottom of the river and got the ring. He gave it to the Curé, who put it on her finger one day after confession. Then she brightened, and waited on and on patiently.

She waited for seven years. Then the deceitful Bénoît came pensively back to her, a cripple from a timber accident. She believed what he told her; and that was where her comedy ended and her tragedy began.

THE MARRIAGE OF
THE MILLER

Medallion put it into his head on the day that Bénoît and Annette were married. "See," said Medallion, "Annette wouldn't have you—and quite right—and she took what was left of that Bénoît, who'll laugh at you over his mush-and-milk."

"Bénoît will want flour someday, with no money." The old man chuckled and rubbed his hands.

"That's nothing; he has the girl—an angel!"

"Good enough, that is what I said of her—an angel!"

"Get married yourself, Farette."

For reply Farette thrust a bag of native *tabac*[34] into Medallion's hands. Then they went over the names of the girls in the village. Medallion objected to those for whom he wished a better future, but

---

[34] Tobacco, presumably from a native (i.e. Indigenous) producer; traditionally tobacco played an important role in many First Nations communities.

they decided at last on Julie Lachance, who, Medallion thought, would in time profoundly increase Farette's respect for the memory of his first wife; for Julie was not an angel. Then the details were ponderously thought out by the miller, and ponderously acted upon, with the dry approval of Medallion, who dared not tell the Curé of his complicity, though he was without compunction. He had a sense of humour, and knew there could be no tragedy in the thing—for Julie. But the miller was a careful man and original in his methods. He still possessed the wardrobe of the first wife, thoughtfully preserved by his sister, even to the wonderful grey watered-poplin which had been her wedding-dress. These he had taken out, shaken free of cayenne, camphor, and lavender, and sent upon the back of Parpon, the dwarf, to the house where Julie lodged (she was an orphan), following himself with a statement on brown paper, showing the extent of his wealth, and a parcel of very fine flour from the new stones in his mill. All was spread out, and then he made a speech, describing his virtues, and condoning his one offence of age by assuring her that every tooth in his head was sound. This was merely the concession of politeness, for he thought his offer handsome.

Julie slyly eyed the wardrobe and as slyly smiled, and then, imitating Farette's manner—though Farette could not see it, and Parpon spluttered with laughter—said:

"M'sieu', you are a great man. The grey poplin is noble, also the flour, and the writing on the brown paper. M'sieu', you go to Mass, and all your teeth are sound; you have a dog-churn, also three feather-beds, and five rag carpets; you have sat on the grand jury.

"M'sieu', I have a *dot*; I accept you. M'sieu', I will keep the brown paper, and the grey poplin, and the flour." Then with a grave elaborate bow, "M'sieu'!"

That was the beginning and end of the courtship. For though Farette came every Sunday evening and smoked by the fire, and looked at Julie as she arranged the details of her dowry, he only chuckled, and now and again struck his thigh and said:

"*Mon Dieu*, the ankle, the eye, the good child, Julie, there!"

Then he would fall to thinking and chuckling again. One day he asked her to make him some potato-cakes of the flour he had given her. Her answer was a catastrophe. She could not cook; she was even ignorant of buttermilk-pudding. He went away overwhelmed, but came back some days afterwards and made another speech. He had laid his plans before Medallion, who approved of them. He prefaced the speech by placing the blank marriage certificate on the table. Then he said that his first wife was such a cook, that when she died he paid for an extra Mass and twelve very fine candles. He called upon Parpon to endorse his words, and Parpon nodded to all he said, but, catching Julie's eye, went off into gurgles of laughter, which he pretended were tears, by smothering his face in his *capote*. "Ma'm'selle," said the miller, "I have thought. Some men go to the Avocat or the Curé with great things; but I have been a pilgrimage, I have sat on the grand jury. There, Ma'm'selle!" His chest swelled, he blew out his cheeks, he pulled Parpon's ear as Napoleon pulled Murat's. "Ma'm'selle, *allons!* Babette, the sister of my first wife—ah! she is a great cook also—well, she was pouring into my plate the soup—there is nothing like pea-soup with a fine lump of pork, and thick molasses for the buckwheat cakes. Ma'm'selle, *allons!* Just then I thought. It is very good; you shall see; you shall learn how to cook.

Babette will teach you. Babette said many things. I got mad and spilt the soup. Ma'm'selle—eh, holy, what a turn has your waist!"

At length he made it clear to her what his plans were, and to each and all she consented; but when he had gone she sat and laughed till she cried, and for the hundredth time took out the brown paper and studied the list of Farette's worldly possessions.

The wedding-day came. Julie performed her last real act of renunciation when, in spite of the protests of her friends, she wore the grey watered-poplin,[35] made modern by her own hands. The wedding-day was the anniversary of Farette's first marriage, and the Curé faltered in the exhortation when he saw that Farette was dressed in complete mourning, even to the crape hat-streamers,[36] as he said, out of respect for the memory of his first wife, and as a kind of tribute to his second. At the wedding-breakfast, where Medallion and Parpon were in high glee, Farette announced that he would take the honeymoon himself, and leave his wife to learn cooking from old Babette.

So he went away alone cheerfully, with hymeneal rice[37] falling in showers on his mourning garments; and his new wife was as cheerful as he, and threw rice also.

She learned how to cook, and in time Farette learned that he had his one true inspiration when he wore mourning at his second marriage.

---

[35] A simple fabric in a plain weave with crosswise ribs that typically gives a corded surface.

[36] Crepe (here spelled "crape") was a traditional fabric used for mourning. Victorian mourning caps were trimmed with short tails, called streamers; this would more typically be worn by a widow than a widower, however.

[37] Rice thrown in celebration of the marriage, like confetti.

MATHURIN

The tale was told to me in the little valley beneath Dalgrothe Mountain one September morning. Far and near one could see the swinging of the flail, and the laughter of a ripe summer was upon the land. There was a little Calvary down by the riverside, where the flax-beaters used to say their prayers in the intervals of their work; and it was just at the foot of this that Angèle Rouvier, having finished her prayer, put her rosary in her pocket, wiped her eyes with the hem of her petticoat, and said to me:

"Ah, dat poor Mathurin, I wipe my tears for him!"

"Tell me all about him, won't you, Madame Angèle? I want to hear *you* tell it," I added hastily, for I saw that she would despise me if I showed ignorance of Mathurin's story. Her sympathy with Mathurin's memory was real, but her pleasure at the compliment I paid her was also real.

"Ah! It was ver' longtime ago—yes. My gran'mudder she remember dat Mathurin ver' well. He is not ver' big man. He has a

face—oh, not ver' handsome, not so more handsome as yours—*non!*
His clothes, dey hang on him all loose; his hair, it is all some grey,
and it blow about him head. He is clean to de face, no beard—no,
nosing like dat. But his eye—là, M'sieu', his eye! It is like a coal which
you blow in your hand, whew!—all bright. My gran'mudder, she say,
'*Voilà*, you can light your pipe with de eyes of dat Mathurin!' She
know. She say dat M'sieu' Mathurin's eyes dey shine in de dark. My
gran'fadder he say he not need any lights on his cariole when
Mathurin ride with him in de night.

"Ah, sure! it is ver' true what I tell you all de time. If you cut off
Mathurin at de chin, all de way up, you will say de top of him it is a
priest. All de way down from his neck, oh, he is just no better as
yoursel' or my Jean—*non!* He is a ver' good man. Only one bad ting
he do. Dat is why I pray for him; dat is why everybody pray for
him—only one bad ting. *Sapristi!*[38]—if I have only one ting to say
God-have-mercy for, I tink dat ver' good; I do my penance happy.
Well, dat Mathurin him use to teach de school. De Curé he ver' fond
of him. All de leetla children, boys and girls, dey all say: '*C'est bon
Mathurin!*' He is not ver' cross—*non!* He have no wife, no child; jes
live by himself all alone. But he is ver' good friends with everybody
in Pontiac. When he go 'long de street, everybody say, 'Ah, dere go
de good Mathurin!' He laugh, he tell story, he smoke leetla tabac, he
take leetla white wine behin' de door; dat is nosing—*non!*

"He have in de parish five, ten, twenty children all call Mathurin;
he is godfadder with dem—yes. So he go about with plenty of sugar
and sticks of candy in his pocket. He never forget once de age of
every leetla child dat call him godfadder. He have a brain dat work

[38] Exclamation along the lines of "good heavens!"; an oath on the Sacred Host, *Sacrum Corpus Christi.*

like a clock. My gran'fadder he say dat Mathurin have a machine in his head. It make de words, make de thoughts, make de fine speech like de Curé, make de gran' poetry—oh, yes!

"When de King of Englan' go to sit on de throne, Mathurin write ver' nice verse to him. And by-and-by dere come to Mathurin a letter—*voilà*, dat is a letter! It have one, two, three, twenty seals; and de King he say to Mathurin: *Merci mille fois, m sieu.'* You are ver' polite. I tank you. I will keep your verses to tell me dat my French subjects are all loyal like M. Mathurin.' Dat is ver' nice, but Mathurin is not proud—*non!* He write six verses for my gran'mudder—*hein!* Dat is something. He write two verses for de King of Englan' and he write six verses for my gran'mudder—you see! He go on so, dis week, dat week, dis year, dat year, all de time.

"Well, by-and-by dere is trouble on Pontiac. It is ver' great trouble. You see dere is a fight 'gainst de King of Englan', and dat is too bad.[39] It is not his fault; he is ver' nice man; it is de bad men who make de laws for de King in Quebec. Well, one day all over de country everybody take him gun, and de leetla bullets, and say, I will fight de soldier of de King of Englan'—like dat. Ver' well, dere was twenty men in Pontiac, ver' nice men—you will find de names cut in a stone on de church; and den, three times as big, you will find Mathurin's name. Ah, dat is de ting! You see, dat rebellion you English call it, we call it de War of de Patriot—de first War of de Patriot, not de second—well, call it what you like, *quelle différence?* The King of Englan' smash him Patriot War all to pieces. Den dere is ten men of de twenty come back to Pontiac ver' sorry. Dey are not happy, nobody are happy. All de wives, dey cry; all de children, dey

[39] The Lower Canada Rebellion (often referred to as the Patriots' War) of 1837.

are afraid. Some people say, What fools you are; others say, You are no good; but everybody in him heart is ver' sorry all de time.

"Ver' well, by-and-by dere come to Pontiac what you call a colonel with a dozen men—what for, you tink? To try de patriots. He will stan' dem against de wall and shoot dem to death—kill dem dead. When dey come, de Curé he is not in Pontiac—*non*, not dat day; he is gone to anudder village. De English soldier he has de ten men drew up before de church. All de children and all de wives dey cry and cry, and dey feel so bad. Certainlee, it is a pity. But de English soldier he say he will march dem off to Quebec, and everybody know dat is de end of de patriots.

"All at once de colonel's horse it grow ver' wild, it rise up high, and dance on him hind feet, and—*voilà!* he topple him over backwards, and de horse fall on de colonel and smaish him—smaish him till he go to die. Ver' well; de colonel, what does he do? Dey lay him on de steps of de church. Den he say: 'Bring me a priest, quick, for I go to die.' Nobody answer. De colonel he say: 'I have a hunder sins all on my mind; dey are on my heart like a hill. Bring to me de priest,'—he groan like dat. Nobody speak at first; den somebody say de priest is not here. 'Find me a priest,' say de colonel; 'find me a priest.' For he tink de priest will not come, becos' he go to kill de patriots. 'Bring me a priest,' he say again, 'and all de ten shall go free.' He say it over and over. He is smaish to pieces, but his head is all right. All at once de doors of de church open behin' him—what you tink! Everybody's heart it stan' still, for dere is Mathurin dress as de priest, with a leetla boy to swing de censer. Everybody say to himself, What is dis? Mathurin is dress as de priest—ah! dat is a sin. It is what you call blasphème.

"The English soldier he look up at Mathurin and say: 'Ah, a priest at last—ah, M'sieu' le Curé, comfort me!'

Mathurin look down on him and say: 'M'sieu', it is for you to confess your sins, and to have de office of de Church. But first, as you have promise just now, you must give up dese poor men, who have fight for what dey tink is right. You will let dem go free dis momen'?'

'Yes, yes,' say de English colonel; 'dey shall go free. Only give me de help of de Church at my last.'

Mathurin turn to de other soldiers and say: 'Unloose de men.'

"De colonel nod his head and say: 'Unloose de men.' Den de men are unloose, and dey all go away, for Mathurin tell dem to go quick.

"Everybody is ver' 'fraid becos' of what Mathurin do. Mathurin he say to de soldiers: 'Lift him up and bring him in de church.' Dey bring him up to de steps of de altar. Mathurin look at de man for a while, and it seem as if he cannot speak to him; but de colonel say: 'I have give you my word. Give me comfort of de Church before I die.' He is in ver' great pain, so Mathurin he turn roun' to everybody dat stan' by, and tell dem to say de prayers for de sick. Everybody get him down on his knees and say de prayer. Everybody say: *Lord have mercy. Spare him, O Lord; deliver him, O Lord, from Thy wrath.'* And Mathurin he pray all de same as a priest, ver' soft and gentle. He pray on and on, and de face of de English soldier it get ver' quiet and still, and de tear drop down his cheek. And just as Mathurin say at de last his sins dey are forgive, he die. Den Mathurin, as he go away to take off his robes, he say to himself: *'Miserere meî Deus!*[40] *miserere meî Deus.'*

"So dat is de ting dat Mathurin do to save de patriots from de bullets. Ver' well, de men dey go free, and when de Governor at

[40] "Have mercy on me, O God!"

Quebec he hear de truth, he say it is all right. Also de English soldier die in peace and happy, becos' he tink his sins are forgive. But den— dere is Mathurin and his sin to pretend he is a priest! The Curé he come back, and dere is a great trouble.

"Mathurin he is ver' quiet and still. Nobody come near him in him house; nobody go near to de school. But he sit alone all day in de school, and he work on de blackboar' and he write on de slate; but dere is no child come, becos' de Curé has forbid any one to speak to Mathurin. Not till de next Sunday, den de Curé send for Mathurin to come to de church. Mathurin come to de steps of de altar; den de Curé say to him:

"'Mathurin, you have sin a great sin. If it was two hunderd years ago you would be put to death for dat.'

"Mathurin he say ver' soft: 'Dat is no matter. I am ready to die now. I did it to save de fadders of de children and de husbands of de wives. I do it to make a poor sinner happy as he go from de world. De sin is mine.'

"Den de Curé he say: 'De men are free, dat is good; de wives have dere husbands and de children dere fadders. Also de man who confess his sins—de English soldier—to whom you say de words of a priest of God, he is forgive. De Spirit of God it was upon him when he die, becos' you speak in de name of de Church. But for you, blasphemer, who take upon you de holy ting, you shall suffer! For penance, all your life you shall teach a chile no more.'

"Voila, M'sieu' le Curé he know dat is de greatest penance for de poor Mathurin! Den he set him other tings to do; and every month for a whole year Mathurin come on his knees all de way to de church, but de Curé say: 'Not yet are you forgive.' At de end of de year Mathurin he look so thin, so white, you can blow through him.

Every day he go to him school and write on de blackboar', and mark on de slate, and call de roll of de school. But dere is no answer, for dere is no children. But all de time de wives of de men dat he have save, and de children, dey pray for him. And by-and-by all de village pray for him, so sorry.

"It is so for two years; and den dey say dat Mathurin he go to die. He cannot come on his knees to de church; and de men whose life he save, dey come to de Curé and ask him to take de penance from Mathurin. De Curé say: 'Wait till nex' Sunday.' So nex' Sunday Mathurin is carry to de church—he is too weak to walk on his knees. De Curé he stan' at de altar, and he read a letter from de Pope, which say dat Mathurin his penance is over, and he is forgive; dat de Pope himself pray for Mathurin, to save his soul. So Mathurin, all at once he stan' up, and his face it smile and smile, and he stretch out his arms as if dey are on a cross, and he say, 'Lord, I am ready to go,' and he fall down. But de Curé catch him as he fall, and Mathurin say: 'De children—let dem come to me dat I teach dem before I die.' And all de children in de church dey come close to him, and he sit up and smile at dem, and he say:

"'It is de class in 'rithmetic. How much is three times four?' And dem all answer: 'T'ree times four is twelve.' And he say: 'May de Twelve Apostles pray for me!' Den he ask: 'Class in geography—how far is it roun' de world?' And dey answer: 'Twenty-four t'ousand miles.' He say: 'Good; it is not so far to God! De school is over all de time,' he say. And dat is only everything of poor Mathurin. He is dead.

"When de Curé lay him down, after he make de Sign upon him, he kiss his face and say: 'Mathurin, now you are a priest unto God.'"

That was Angèle Rouvier's story of Mathurin, the Master of the School, for whom the women and the children pray in the parish of Pontiac, though the school has been dismissed these hundred years and more.

THE STORY OF THE LIME BURNER

For a man in whose life there had been tragedy he was cheerful. He had a habit of humming vague notes in the silence of conversation, as if to put you at your ease. His body and face were lean and arid, his eyes oblique and small, his hair straight and dry and straw-coloured; and it flew out crackling with electricity, to meet his cap as he put it on. He lived alone in a little hut near his lime-kiln by the river, with no near neighbours, and few companions save his four dogs; and these he fed sometimes at expense of his own stomach. He had just enough crude poetry in his nature to enjoy his surroundings. For he was well placed. Behind the lime-kiln rose knoll on knoll, and beyond these the verdant hills, all converging to Dalgrothe Mountain. In front of it was the river, with its banks dropping forty feet, and below, the rapids, always troubled and sportive. On the farther side of the river lay peaceful areas of meadow and corn land, and low-roofed, hovering farm-houses, with one larger than the rest, having a wind-mill and a flag-staff. This building was almost large enough for a manor, and indeed it was said that it had been built for one just before the conquest in 1759,[41] but the war had destroyed the ambitious owner, and it had become a farm-house. Paradis always knew the time of the day by the way the light fell on the wind-mill. He had owned this farm once, he and his brother Fabian, and he had loved it as he loved Fabian, and he loved it now as he loved Fabian's memory. In spite of all, they were cheerful memories, both of brother and house.

At twenty-three they had become orphans, with two hundred acres of land, some cash, horses and cattle, and plenty of credit in the parish, or in the county, for that matter. Both were of hearty dispositions, but Fabian had a taste for liquor, and Henri for pretty faces and shapely ankles. Yet no one thought the worse of them for that, especially at first. An old servant kept house for them and cared for them in her honest way, both physically and morally. She lectured them when at first there was little to lecture about. It is no wonder that when there came a vast deal to reprove, the *bonne*[42] desisted altogether, overwhelmed by the weight of it.

Henri got a shock the day before their father died when he saw Fabian lift the brandy used to mix with the milk of the dying man, and pouring out the third of a tumbler, drink it off, smacking his lips as he did so, as though it were a cordial. That gave him a cue to his future and to Fabian's. After their father died Fabian gave way to the vice. He drank in the taverns, he was at once the despair and the joy of the parish; for, wild as he was, he had a gay temper, a humorous mind, a strong arm, and was the universal lover. The Curé, who did

---

[41] The acquisition of regions of New France by Britain following the Seven Years' War.

[42] Good woman.

not, of course, know one-fourth of his wildness, had a warm spot for him in his heart. But there was a vicious strain in him somewhere, and it came out one day in a perilous fashion.

There was in the hotel of the Louis Quinze an English servant from the west, called Nell Barraway. She had been in a hotel in Montreal, and it was there Fabian had seen her as she waited at table. She was a splendid-looking creature—all life and energy, tall, fair-haired, and with a charm above her kind. She was also an excellent servant, could do as much as any two women in any house, and was capable of more airy *diablerie* than any ten of her sex in Pontiac. When Fabian had said to her in Montreal that he would come to see her again, he told her where he lived. She came to see him instead, for she wrote to the landlord of the Louis Quinze, enclosed fine testimonials, and was at once engaged. Fabian was stunned when he entered the Louis Quinze and saw her waiting at table, alert, busy, good to behold. She nodded at him with a quick smile as he stood bewildered just inside the door, then said in English: "This way, m'sieu'."

As he sat down he said in English also, with a laugh and with snapping eyes: "Good Lord, what brings you here, lady-bird?"

As she pushed a chair under him she whispered through his hair: "You!" and then was gone away to fetch pea-soup for six hungry men.

The Louis Quinze did more business now in three months than it had done before in six. But it became known among a few in Pontiac that Nell was notorious. How it had crept up from Montreal no one guessed, and, when it did come, her name was very intimately associated with Fabian's. No one could say that she was not the most perfect of servants, and also no one could say that her life in Pontiac had not been exemplary. Yet wise people had made up their minds that she was determined to marry Fabian, and the wisest declared that she would do so in spite of everything—religion (she was a Protestant), character, race. She was clever, as the young Seigneur found, as the little Avocat was forced to admit, as the Curé allowed with a sigh, and she had no airs of badness at all and very little of usual coquetry. Fabian was enamoured, and it was clear that he intended to bring the woman to the Manor one way or another.

Henri admitted the fascination of the woman, felt it, despaired, went to Montreal, got proof of her career, came back, and made his final and only effort to turn his brother from the girl.

He had waited an hour outside the hotel for his brother, and when Fabian got in, he drove on without a word. After a while, Fabian, who was in high spirits, said:

"Open your mouth, Henri. Come along, sleepyhead."

Straightway he began to sing a rollicking song, and Henri joined in with him heartily, for the spirit of Fabian's humour was contagious:

> "There was a little man,
> The foolish Guilleri
> Carabi.
> He went unto the chase,
> Of partridges the chase.
> Carabi.
> Titi Carabi,
> Toto Carabo,
> You're going to break your neck,
> My lovely Guilleri!"

He was about to begin another verse when Henri stopped him, saying:

"You're going to break your neck, Fabian."

"What's up, Henri?" was the reply.

"You're drinking hard, and you don't keep good company."

Fabian laughed. "Can't get the company I want, so what I can get I have, Henri, my lad."

"Don't drink." Henri laid his freehand on Fabian's knee.

"Whiskey-wine is meat and drink to me—I was born on New Year's Day, old coffin-face. Whiskey-wine day, they ought to call it. Holy! the empty jars that day." Henri sighed. "That's the drink, Fabian," he said patiently. "Give up the company. I'll be better company for you than that girl, Fabian."

"Girl? What the devil do you mean!"

"She, Nell Barraway, was the company I meant, Fabian."

"Nell Barraway—you mean her? Bosh! I'm going to marry her, Henri."

"You mustn't, Fabian," said Henri, eagerly clutching Fabian's sleeve.

"But I must, my Henri. She's the best-looking, wittiest girl I ever saw—splendid. Never lonely with her."

"Looks and brains isn't everything, Fabian."

"Isn't it, though? Isn't it? *Tiens*, you try it!"

"Not without goodness." Henri's voice weakened.

"That's bosh. Of course it is, Henri, my dear. If you love a woman, if she gets hold of you, gets into your blood, loves you so that the touch of her fingers sets your pulses going *pom-pom*, you don't care a sou[43] whether she is good or not."

"You mean whether she was good or not?"

"No, I don't. I mean is good or not. For if she loves you she'll travel straight for your sake. Pshaw, you don't know anything about it!"

"I know all about it."

"Know all about it! You're in love—you?"

"Yes."

Fabian sat open-mouthed for a minute. "Godam!" he said. It was his one English oath.

"Is she good company?" he asked after a minute.

"She's the same as you keep—voilà, the same."

"You mean Nell—Nell?" asked Fabian, in a dry, choking voice.

"Yes, Nell. From the first time I saw her. But I'd cut my hand off first. I'd think of you; of our people that have been here for two hundred years; of the rooms in the old house where mother used to be."

Fabian laughed nervously. "Holy heaven, and you've got her in your blood, too!"

"Yes, but I'd never marry her. Fabian, at Montreal I found out all about her. She was as bad—"

"That's nothing to me, Henri," said Fabian, "but something else is. Here you are now. I'll make a bargain." His face showed pale in the moonlight. "If you'll drink with me, do as I do, go where I go, play the devil when I play it, and never squeal, never hang back, I'll give her up. But I've got to have you—got to have you all the time, everywhere, hunting, drinking, or letting alone. You'll see me out,

<hr />

[43] Cent or penny.

for you're stronger, had less of it. I'm soon for the little low house in the grass. Stop the horses."

Henri stopped them and they got out. They were just opposite the lime-kiln, and they had to go a few hundred yards before they came to the bridge to cross the river to their home. The light of the fire shone in their faces as Fabian handed the flask to Henri, and said: "Let's drink to it, Henri. You half, and me half." He was deadly pale.

Henri drank to the finger-mark set, and then Fabian lifted the flask to his lips.

"Good-bye, Nell!" he said. "Here's to the good times we've had!" He emptied the flask, and threw it over the bank into the burning lime, and Garotte, the old lime-burner, being half asleep, did not see or hear.

The next day the two went on a long hunting expedition, and the following month Nell Barraway left for Montreal.

Henri kept to his compact, drink for drink, sport for sport. One year the crops were sold before they were reaped, horses and cattle went little by little, then came mortgage, and still Henri never wavered, never weakened, in spite of the Curé and all others. The brothers were always together, and never from first to last did Henri lose his temper, or openly lament that ruin was coming surely on them. What money Fabian wanted he got. The Curé's admonitions availed nothing, for Fabian would go his gait. The end came on the very spot where the compact had been made; for, passing the lime-kiln one dark night, as the two rode home together, Fabian's horse shied, the bank of the river gave way, and with a startled 'Ah, Henri." the profligate and his horse were gone into the river below.

Next month the farm and all were sold, Henri Paradis succeeded the old lime-burner at his post, drank no more ever, and lived his life in sight of the old home.

THE WOODSMAN'S STORY OF THE GREAT WHITE CHIEF

The old woodsman shifted the knife with which he was mending his fishing-rod from one hand to the other, and looked at it musingly, before he replied to Medallion. "Yes, m'sieu', I knew the White Chief, as they called him: this was his"—holding up the knife; "and this"—taking a watch from his pocket. "He gave them to me; I was with him in the Circle on the great journey."

"Tell us about him, then," Medallion urged; "for there are many tales, and who knows which is the right one?"

"The right one is mine. Holy, he was to me like a father then! I know more of the truth than any one." He paused a moment, looking out on the river where the hot sun was playing with all its might, then took off his cap with deliberation, laid it beside him, and speaking as it were into the distance, began:

"He once was a trader of the Hudson's Bay Company.[44] Of his birth some said one thing, some another; I know he was *beaucoup gentil,* and his heart, it was a lion's! Once, when there was trouble with the Chipp'ways,[45] he went alone to their camp, and say he will fight their strongest man, to stop the trouble. He twist the neck of the great fighting man of the tribe, so that it go with a snap, and that ends it, and he was made a chief, for, you see, in their hearts they all hated their strong man. Well, one winter there come down to Fort o' God two Esquimaux, and they say that three white men are wintering by the Coppermine River; they had travel down from the frozen seas when their ship was lock in the ice, but can get no farther. They were sick with the evil skin,[46] and starving. The White Chief say to me: 'Galloir, will you go to rescue them?' I would have gone with him to the ends of the world—and this was near one end."

The old man laughed to himself, tossed his jet-black hair from his wrinkled face, and after a moment, went on: "There never was such a winter as that. The air was so still by times that you can hear the rustle of the stars and the shifting of the northern lights; but the cold at night caught you by the heart and clamp it—*Mon Dieu,* how it clamp! We crawl under the snow and lay in our bags of fur and wool, and the dogs hug close to us. We were sorry for the dogs; and one died, and then another, and there is nothing so dreadful as to hear the dogs howl in the long night—it is like ghosts crying in an

---

[44] The oldest commercial corporation in North America (and one of the oldest in the world), the Hudson's Bay Company was a fur trading business for much of its existence.

[45] The Ojibwe nation (sometimes referred to as Chippewa).

[46] Possibly scurvy, a symptom of which is scaly, dry, and brownish skin.

empty world. The circle of the sun get smaller and smaller, till he only tramp along the high edge of the north-west. We got to the river at last and found the camp. There is one man dead—only one; but there were bones—ah, m'sieu', you not guess what a thing it is to look upon the bones of men, and know *that*—!"

Medallion put his hand on the old man's arm. "Wait a minute," he said. Then he poured out coffee for both, and they drank before the rest was told.

"It's a creepy story," said Medallion, "but go on."

"Well, the White Chief look at the dead man as he sit there in the snow, with a book and a piece of paper beside him, and the pencil in the book. The face is bent forward to the knees. The White Chief pick up the book and pencil, and then kneel down and gaze up in the dead man's face, all hard like stone and crusted with frost. I thought he would never stir again, he look so long. I think he was puzzle. Then he turn and say to me: 'So quiet, so awful, Galloir!' and got up. Well, but it was cold then, and my head seemed big and running about like a ball of air. But I light a spirit-lamp, and make some coffee, and he open the dead man's book—it is what they call a diary—and begin to read. All at once I hear a cry, and I see him drop the book on the ground, and go to the dead man, and jerk his fist as if to strike him in the face. But he did not strike."

Galloir stopped, and lighted his pipe, and was so long silent that Medallion had to jog him into speaking. He puffed the smoke so that his face was in the cloud, and he said through it: "No, he did not strike. He get to his feet and spoke: 'God forgive her!' like that, and come and take up the book again, and read. He eat and drunk, and read the book again, and I know by his face that something more than cold was clamp his heart.

"'Shall we bury him in the snow?' I say. 'No,' he spoke, 'let him sit there till the Judgmen'. This is a wonderful book, Galloir,' he went on. 'He was a brave man, but the rest—the rest!'—then under his breath almost: 'She was so young—but a child.' I not understand that. We start away soon, leaving *the thing* there. For four days, and then I see that the White Chief will never get back to Fort Pentecost; but he read the dead man's book much. . . ."

"I cannot forget that one day. He lies down looking at the world—nothing but the waves of snow, shining blue and white, on and on. The sun lift an eye of blood in the north, winking like a devil as I try to drive Death away by calling in his ear. He wake all at once; but his eyes seem asleep. He tell me to take the book to a great man in Montreal—he give me the name. Then he take out his watch—it is stop—and this knife, and put them into my hands, and then he pat my shoulder. He motion to have the bag drawn over his head. I do it. . . . Of course that was the end!"

"But what about the book?" Medallion asked.

"That book? It is strange. I took it to the man in Montreal—*Tonnerre*,[47] what a fine house and good wine had he!—and told him all. He whip out a scarf, and blow his nose loud, and say very angry: 'So, she's lost both now! What a scoundrel he was! . . .' Which one did he mean? I not understan' ever since."

---

[47] An expletive.

UNCLE JIM

He was no uncle of mine, but it pleased me that he let me call him Uncle Jim.

It seems only yesterday that, for the first time, on a farm "over the border" from the French province, I saw him standing by a log outside the wood-house door, splitting maple knots. He was all bent by years and hard work, with muscles of iron, hands gnarled and lumpy, but clinching like a vise; grey head thrust forward on shoulders which had carried forkfuls of hay and grain, and leaned to the cradle and the scythe, and been heaped with cordwood till they were like hide and metal; white straggling beard and red watery eyes, which, to me, were always hung with an intangible veil of mystery—though that, maybe, was my boyish fancy. Added to all this he was so very deaf that you had to speak clear and loud into his ear; and many people he could not hear at all, if their words were not sharp-cut, no matter how loud. A silent, withdrawn man he was, living close to Mother Earth, twin-brother of Labour, to whom Morning and Daytime were sounding-boards for his axe, scythe, saw, flail, and milking-pail, and Night a round hollow of darkness into which he crept, shutting the doors called Silence behind him, till the impish page of Toil came tapping again, and he stepped awkwardly into the working world once more. Winter and summer saw him putting the kettle on the fire a few minutes after four o'clock, in winter issuing with lantern from the kitchen door to the stable and barn to feed the stock; in summer sniffing the grey dawn and looking out on his fields of rye and barley, before he went to gather the cows for milking and take the horses to water.

For forty years he and his worn-faced wife bowed themselves beneath the yoke, first to pay for the hundred-acre farm, and then to bring up and educate their seven children. Something noble in them gave them ambitions for their boys and girls which they had never had for themselves; but when had gone the forty years, in which the little farm had twice been mortgaged to put the eldest son through college as a doctor, they faced the bitter fact that the farm had passed from them to Rodney, the second son, who had come at last to keep a hotel in a town fifty miles away. Generous-hearted people would think that these grown-up sons and daughters should have returned the old people's long toil and care by buying up the farm and handing it back to them, their rightful refuge in the decline of life. But it was not so. They were tenants where they had been owners, dependants where they had been givers, slaves where once they were masters. The old mother toiled without a servant, the old man without a helper, save in harvest time.

But the great blow came when Rodney married the designing milliner who flaunted her wares opposite his bar-room; and, somehow, from the date of that marriage, Rodney's good fortune and the hotel declined. When he and his wife first visited the little farm after their marriage the old mother shrank away from the young woman's painted face, and ever afterwards an added sadness showed in her bearing and in her patient smile. But she took Rodney's wife through the house, showing her all there was to show, though that was not much. There was the little parlour with its hair-cloth chairs, rag carpet, centre table, and iron stove with black pipes, all gaily varnished. There was the parlour bedroom off it, with the one feather-bed of the house bountifully piled up with coarse home-made blankets, topped by a silk patchwork quilt, the artistic labour of the old wife's evening hours while Uncle Jim peeled apples and strung them to dry from the rafters. There was a room, dining-room in summer, and kitchen dining-room in winter, as clean as aged hands could scrub and dust it, hung about with stray pictures from illustrated papers, and a good old clock in the corner "ticking" life, and youth, and hope away. There was the buttery[48] off that, with its meagre china and crockery, its window looking out on the field of rye, the little orchard of winter apples, and the hedge of cranberry bushes. Upstairs were rooms with no ceilings, where, lying on a corn-husk bed, you reached up and touched the sloping roof, with windows at the end only, facing the buckwheat field, and looking down two miles towards the main road—for the farm was on a concession or side-road, dusty in summer, and in winter sometimes impassable for weeks together. It was not much of a home, as any one with the mind's eye can see, but four stalwart men and three fine women had been born, raised, and quartered there, until, with good clothes, and speaking decent English and tolerable French, and with

---

[48] A service room for storing goods (often alcohol in "butts" or barrels), usually off the main hall in a medieval house.

money in their pockets, hardly got by the old people, one by one they issued forth into the world.

The old mother showed Rodney's wife what there was for eyes to see, not forgetting the three hives of bees on the south side, beneath the parlour window. She showed it with a kind of pride, for it all seemed good to her, and every dish, and every chair, and every corner in the little house had to her a glory of its own, because of those who had come and gone—the firstlings of her flock, the roses of her little garden of love, blooming now in a rougher air than ranged over the little house on the hill. She had looked out upon the pine woods to the east and the meadow-land to the north, the sweet valley between the rye-field and the orchard, and the good honest air that had blown there for forty years, bracing her heart and body for the battle of love and life, and she had said through all, Behold it is very good.

But the pert milliner saw nothing of all this; she did not stand abashed in the sacred precincts of a home where seven times the Angel of Death had hovered over a birth-bed. She looked into the face which Time's finger had anointed, and motherhood had etched with trouble, and said:

" 'Tisn't much, is it? Only a clap-board house, and no ceilings upstairs, and rag carpets—pshaw!"

And when she came to wash her hands for dinner, she threw aside the unscented, common bar-soap, and, shrugging her narrow shoulders at the coarse towel, wiped her fingers on her cambric handkerchief. Any other kind of a woman, when she saw the old mother going about with her twisted wrist—a doctor's bad work with a fracture—would have tucked up her dress, and tied on an apron to help. But no, she sat and preened herself with the tissue-paper sort of pride of a vain milliner, or nervously shifted about, lifting up this and that, curiously supercilious, her tongue rattling on to her husband and to his mother in a shallow, foolish way. She couldn't say, however, that anything was out of order or ill-kept about the place. The old woman's rheumatic fingers made corners clean, and wood as white as snow, the stove was polished, the tins were bright, and her own dress, no matter what her work, neat as a girl's, although the old graceful poise of the body had twisted out of drawing.

But the real crisis came when Rodney, having stood at the wood-house door and blown the dinner-horn as he used to do when a boy, the sound floating and crying away across the rye-field, the old man came—for, strange to say, that was the one sound he could hear easily, though, as he said to himself, it seemed as small as a pin, coming from ever so far away. He came heavily up from the barn-yard, mopping his red face and forehead, and now and again raising his hand to shade his eyes, concerned to see the unknown visitors, whose horse and buggy were in the stable-yard. He and Rodney greeted outside warmly enough, but there was some trepidation too in Uncle Jim's face—he felt trouble brewing; and there is no trouble like that which comes between parent and child. Silent as he was, however, he had a large and cheerful heart, and nodding his head he laughed the deep, quaint laugh which Rodney himself of all his sons had—and he was fonder of Rodney than any. He washed his hands in the little basin outside the wood-house door, combed out his white beard, rubbed his red, watery eyes, tied a clean handkerchief round his neck, put on a rusty but clean old coat, and a minute afterwards was shaking hands for the first time with Rodney's wife. He had lived much apart from his kind, but he had a mind that fastened upon a thought and worked it down until it was an axiom. He felt how shallow was this thin, flaunting woman of flounces and cheap rouge; he saw her sniff at the brown sugars—she had always had white at the hotel; and he noted that she let Rodney's mother clear away and wash the dinner things herself. He felt the little crack of doom before it came.

It came about three o'clock. He did not return to the rye-field after dinner, but stayed and waited to hear what Rodney had to say. Rodney did not tell his little story well, for he foresaw trouble in the old home; but he had to face this and all coming dilemmas as best he might. With a kind of shamefacedness, yet with an attempt to carry the thing off lightly, he told Uncle Jim, while, inside, his wife told the old mother, that the business of the hotel had gone to pot (he did not say who was the cause of that), and they were selling out to his partner and coming to live on the farm.

"I'm tired anyway of the hotel job," said Rodney. "Farming's a better life. Don't you think so, dad?"

"It's better for me, Rod," answered Uncle Jim, "it's better for me."

Rodney was a little uneasy. "But won't it be better for me?" he asked.

"Mebbe," was the slow answer, "mebbe, mebbe so."

"And then there's mother, she's getting too old for the work, ain't she?"

"She's done it straight along," answered the old man, "straight along till now."

"But Millie can help her, and we'll have a hired girl, eh?"

"I dunno, I dunno," was the brooding answer; "the place ain't going to stand it."

"We'll get more out of it," answered Rodney. "I'll stock it up, I'll put more under barley. All the thing wants is working, dad. Put more in, get more out. Now ain't that right?"

The other was looking off towards the rye-field, where, for forty years, up and down the hillside, he had travelled with the cradle and the scythe, putting all there was in him into it, and he answered, blinking along the avenue of the past:

"Mebbe, mebbe!"

Rodney fretted under the old man's vague replies, and said: "But darn it all, can't you tell us what you think?"

His father did not take his eyes off the rye-field. "I'm thinking," he answered, in the same old-fashioned way, "that I've been working here since you were born, Rod. I've blundered along, somehow, just boggling my way through. I ain't got anything more to say. The farm ain't mine any more, but I'll keep my scythe sharp and my axe ground just as I always did, and I'm for workin' as I've always worked as long as I'm let to stay."

"Good Lord, dad, don't talk that way! Things ain't going to be any different for you and mother than they are now. Only, of course—" He paused.

The old man pieced out the sentence: "Only, of course, there can't be two women rulin' one house, Rod, and you know it as well as I do."

Exactly how Rodney's wife told the old mother of the great change Rodney never knew; but when he went back to the house the grey look in his mother's face told him more than her words ever told. Before they left that night the pink milliner had already planned the changes which were to celebrate her coming and her ruling.

So Rodney and his wife came, all the old man prophesied in a few brief sentences to his wife proving true. There was no great struggle on the mother's part; she stepped aside from governing, and became as like a servant as could be. An insolent servant-girl came, and she and Rodney's wife started a little drama of incompetency, which should end as the hotel-keeping ended. Wastefulness, cheap luxury, tawdry living, took the place of the old, frugal, simple life. But the mother went about with that unchanging sweetness of face, and a body withering about a fretted soul. She had no bitterness, only a miserable distress. But every slight that was put upon her, every change, every new-fangled idea, from the white sugar to the scented soap and the yellow buggy, rankled in the old man's heart. He had resentment both for the old wife and himself, and he hated the pink milliner for the humiliation that she heaped upon them both. Rodney did not see one-fifth of it, and what he did see lost its force, because, strangely enough, he loved the gaudy wife who wore gloves on her bloodless hands as she did the house-work and spent numberless afternoons in trimming her own bonnets. Her peevishness grew apace as the newness of the experience wore off. Uncle Jim seldom spoke to her, as he seldom spoke to anybody, but she had an inkling of the rancour in his heart, and many a time she put blame upon his shoulders to her husband, when some unavoidable friction came.

A year, two years, passed, which were as ten upon the shoulders of the old people, and then, in the dead of winter, an important thing happened. About the month of March Rodney's first child was expected. At the end of January Rodney had to go away, expecting to return in less than a month. But, in the middle of February, the woman's sacred trouble[49] came before its time. And on that day there fell such a storm as had not been seen for many a year. The concession road was blocked before day had well set in; no horse could go ten yards in it. The nearest doctor was miles away at Pontiac, and for any man to face the journey was to connive with death. The old mother came to Uncle Jim, and, as she looked out of a little unfrosted spot on the window at the blinding storm, told him that the pink milliner would die. There seemed to be no other end to it, for the chances were a hundred to one against the strongest man making a journey for the doctor, and another hundred to one against the doctor's coming.

No one knows whether Uncle Jim could hear the cries from the torture-chamber, but, after standing for a time mumbling to himself, he wrapped himself in a heavy coat, tied a muffler about his face, and went out. If they missed him they must have thought him gone to the barn, or in the drive-shed sharpening his axe. But the day went on and the old mother forgot all the wrongs that she had suffered, and yearned over the trivial woman who was hurrying out into the Great Space. Her hours seemed numbered at noon, her moments measured as it came towards sundown, but with the passing of the sun the storm stopped, and a beautiful white peace fell on the world of snow, and suddenly out of that peace came six men; and the first that opened the door was the doctor. After him came Uncle Jim, supported between two others.

Uncle Jim had made the terrible journey, falling at last in the streets of the county town with frozen hands and feet, not a dozen rods from the doctor's door. They brought him to, he told his story, and, with the abating of the storm, the doctor and the villagers drove

---

[49] Childbirth; here a premature labour.

down to the concession road, and then made their way slowly up across the fields, carrying the old man with them, for he would not be left behind.

An hour after the doctor entered the parlour bedroom the old mother came out to where the old man sat, bundled up beside the fire with bandaged hands and feet.

"She's safe, Jim, and the child too," she said softly. The old man twisted in his chair, and blinked into the fire. "Dang my soul!" he said.

The old woman stooped and kissed his grey tangled hair. She did not speak, and she did not ask him what he meant; but there and then they took up their lives again and lived them out.

THE HOUSE WITH
THE TALL PORCH

No one ever visited the House except the Little Chemist, the Avocat, and Medallion; and Medallion, though merely an auctioneer, was the only person on terms of intimacy with its owner, the old Seigneur, who for many years had never stirred beyond the limits of his little garden. At rare intervals he might be seen sitting in the large stone porch which gave overweighted dignity to the house, itself not very large.

An air of mystery surrounded the place: in summer the grass was rank, the trees seemed huddled together in gloom about the houses, the vines appeared to ooze on the walls, and at one end, where the window-shutters were always closed and barred, a great willow drooped and shivered; in winter the stone walls showed naked and grim among the gaunt trees and furtive shrubs.

None who ever saw the Seigneur could forget him—a tall figure with stooping shoulders; a pale, deeply lined, clean-shaven face, and a forehead painfully white, with blue veins showing; the eyes handsome, penetrative, brooding, and made indescribably sorrowful by the dark skin around them. There were those in Pontiac, such as the Curé, who remembered when the Seigneur was constantly to be seen in the village; and then another person was with him always, a tall, handsome youth, his son. They were fond and proud of each other, and were religious and good citizens in a highbred, punctilious way.

At that time the Seigneur was all health and stalwart strength. But one day a rumour went abroad that he had quarrelled with his son because of the wife of Farette the miller. No one outside knew if the thing was true, but Julie, the miller's wife, seemed rather to plume herself that she had made a stir in her little world. Yet the curious habitants came to know that the young man had gone, and after a few years his having once lived there had become a mere memory. But whenever the Little Chemist set foot inside the tall porch he remembered; the Avocat was kept in mind by papers which he was called upon to read and alter from time to time; the Curé never forgot, because when the young man went he lost not one of his flock but two; and Medallion, knowing something of the story, had wormed a deal of truth out of the miller's wife. Medallion knew that the closed, barred rooms were the young man's; and he knew also that the old man was waiting, waiting, in a hope which he never even named to himself.

One day the silent old housekeeper came rapping at Medallion's door, and simply said to him: "Come—the Seigneur!"

Medallion went, and for hours sat beside the Seigneur's chair, while the Little Chemist watched and sighed softly in a corner, now and again rising to feel the sick man's pulse or to prepare a cordial. The housekeeper hovered behind the high-backed chair, and when the Seigneur dropped his handkerchief—now, as always, of the exquisite fashion of a past century—she put it gently in his hand.

Once when the Little Chemist touched his wrist, his dark eyes rested on him with inquiry, and he said: "Soon?"

It was useless trying to shirk the persistency of that look. "Eight hours, perhaps, sir," the Little Chemist answered, with painful shyness.

The Seigneur seemed to draw himself up a little, and his hand grasped his handkerchief tightly for an instant; then he said: "Soon. Thank you."

After a little, his eyes turned to Medallion and he seemed about to speak, but still kept silent. His chin dropped on his breast, and for a time he was motionless and shrunken; but still there was a strange little curl of pride—or disdain—on his lips. At last he drew up his head, his shoulders came erect, heavily, to the carved back of the chair, where, strange to say, the Stations of the Cross were figured, and he said, in a cold, ironical voice: "The Angel of Patience has lied!"

The evening wore on, and there was no sound, save the ticking of the clock, the beat of rain upon the windows, and the deep breathing of the Seigneur. Presently he started, his eyes opened wide, and his whole body seemed to listen.

"I heard a voice," he said.

"No one spoke, my master," said the housekeeper.

"It was a voice without," he said.

"Monsieur," said the Little Chemist, "it was the wind in the eaves."

His face was almost painfully eager and sensitively alert.

"Hush!" he said; "I hear a voice in the tall porch."

"Sir," said Medallion, laying a hand respectfully on his arm, "it is nothing."

With a light on his face and a proud, trembling energy, he got to his feet. "It is the voice of my son," he said. "Go—go, and bring him in."

No one moved. But he was not to be disobeyed.

His ears had been growing keener as he neared the subtle atmosphere of that Brink where man strips himself to the soul for a lonely voyaging, and he waved the woman to the door.

"Wait," he said, as her hand fluttered at the handle. "Take him to another room. Prepare a supper such as we used to have. When it is ready I will come. But, listen, and obey. Tell him not that I have but four hours of life. Go, good woman, and bring him in."

It was as he said. They found the son weak and fainting, fallen within the porch—a worn, bearded man, returned from failure and suffering and the husks of evil. They clothed him and cared for him, and strengthened him with wine, while the woman wept over him and at last set him at the loaded, well-lighted table. Then the Seigneur came in, leaning his arm very lightly on that of Medallion with a kind of kingly air; and, greeting his son before them all, as if they had parted yesterday, sat down. For an hour they sat there, and the Seigneur talked gaily with a colour to his face, and his great eyes glowing. At last he rose, lifted his glass, and said: "The Angel of Patience is wise. I drink to my son!"

He was about to say something more, but a sudden whiteness passed over his face. He drank off the wine, and as he put the glass down, shivered, and fell back in his chair.

"Two hours short, Chemist!" he said, and smiled, and was Still.

PARPON THE DWARF

Parpon perched in a room at the top of the mill. He could see every house in the village, and he knew people a long distance off. He was a droll dwarf, and, in his way, had good times in the world. He turned the misery of the world into a game, and grinned at it from his high little eyrie with the dormer window. He had lived with Farette the miller for some years, serving him with a kind of humble insolence.

It was not a joyful day for Farette when he married Julie. She led him a pretty travel. He had started as her master; he ended by being her slave and victim. She was a wilful wife. She had made the Seigneur de la Rivière, of the House with the Tall Porch, to quarrel with his son Armand, so that Armand disappeared from Pontiac for years.

When that happened she had already stopped confessing to the good Curé; so it may be guessed there were things she did not care to tell, and for which she had no repentance. But Parpon knew, and

181

Medallion the auctioneer guessed; and the Little Chemist's wife hoped that it was not so. When Julie looked at Parpon, as he perched on a chest of drawers, with his head cocked and his eyes blinking, she knew that he read the truth. But she did not know all that was in his head; so she said sharp things to him, as she did to everybody, for she had a very poor opinion of the world, and thought all as flippant as herself. She took nothing seriously; she was too vain. Except that she was sorry Armand was gone, she rather plumed herself on having separated the Seigneur and his son—it was something to have been the pivot in a tragedy. There came others to the village, as, for instance, a series of clerks to the Avocat; but she would not decline from Armand upon them. She merely made them miserable.

But she did not grow prettier as time went on. Even Annette, the sad wife of the drunken Bénoît, kept her fine looks; but then, Annette's life was a thing for a book, and she had a beautiful child. You cannot keep this from the face of a woman. Nor can you keep the other: when the heart rusts the rust shows.

After a good many years, Armand de la Rivière came back in time to see his father die. Then Julie picked out her smartest ribbons, capered at the mirror, and dusted her face with oatmeal, because she thought that he would ask her to meet him at the Bois Noir, as he had done long ago. The days passed, and he did not come. When she saw Armand at the funeral—a tall man with a dark beard and a grave face, not like the Armand she had known, he seemed a great distance from her, though she could almost have touched him once as he turned from the grave. She would have liked to throw herself into his arms, and cry before them all: *'Mon Armand!'* and go away with him to the House with the Tall Porch. She did not care about Farette, the mumbling old man who hungered for money, having ceased to hunger for anything else—even for Julie, who laughed and shut her door in his face, and cowed him.

After the funeral Julie had a strange feeling. She had not much brains, but she had some shrewdness, and she felt her romance askew. She stood before the mirror, rubbing her face with oatmeal and frowning hard. Presently a voice behind her said: "Madame Julie, shall I bring another bag of meal?"

She turned quickly, and saw Parpon on a table in the corner, his legs drawn up to his chin, his black eyes twinkling.

"Idiot!" she cried, and threw the meal at him. He had a very long, quick arm. He caught the basin as it came, but the meal covered him. He blew it from his beard, laughing softly, and twirled the basin on a finger-point.

"Like that, there will need two bags!" he said.

"Imbecile!" she cried, standing angry in the centre of the room.

"Ho, ho! what a big word! See what it is to have the tongue of fashion!"

She looked helplessly round the room.

"I will kill you!"

"Let us die together," answered Parpon; "we are both sad."

She snatched the poker from the fire, and ran at him. He caught her wrists with his great hands, big enough for tall Medallion, and held her.

"I said 'together,'" he chuckled; "not one before the other. We might jump into the flume at the mill, or go over the dam at the Bois Noir; or, there is Farette's musket which he is cleaning—gracious, but it will kick when it fires, it is so old!"

She sank to the floor. "Why does he clean the musket?" she asked; fear, and something wicked too, in her eye. Her fingers ran forgetfully through the hair on her forehead, pushing it back, and the marks of small-pox showed. The contrast with her smooth cheeks gave her a weird look. Parpon got quickly on the table again and sat like a Turk, with a furtive eye on her. "Who can tell!" he said at last. "That musket has not been fired for years. It would not kill a bird; the shot would scatter: but it might kill a man—a man is bigger."

"Kill a man!" She showed her white teeth with a savage little smile.

"Of course it is all guess. I asked Farette what he would shoot, and he said, 'Nothing good to eat.' I said I would eat what he killed. Then he got pretty mad, and said I couldn't eat my own head. Holy! that was funny for Farette. Then I told him there was no good going to the Bois Noir, for there would be nothing to shoot. Well, did I speak true, Madame Julie?"

She was conscious of something new in Parpon. She could not define it. Presently she got to her feet and said: "I don't believe you— you're a monkey."

"A monkey can climb a tree quick; a man has to take the shot as it comes." He stretched up his powerful arms, with a swift motion as of climbing, laughed, and added: "Madame Julie, Farette has poor eyes; he could not see a hole in a ladder. But he has a kink in his head about the Bois Noir. People have talked—"

"Pshaw!" Julie said, crumpling her apron and throwing it out; "he is a child and a coward. He should not play with a gun; it might go off and hit him."

Parpon hopped down and trotted to the door. Then he turned and said, with a sly gurgle: "Farette keeps at that gun. What is the good! There will be nobody at the Bois Noir any more. I will go and tell him."

She rushed at him with fury, but seeing Annette Bénoît in the road, she stood still and beat her foot angrily on the doorstep. She was ripe for a quarrel, and she would say something hateful to Annette; for she never forgot that Farette had asked Annette to be his wife before herself was considered. She smoothed out her wrinkled apron and waited.

"Good day, Annette," she said loftily.

"Good day, Julie," was the quiet reply.

"Will you come in?"

"I am going to the mill for flax-seed. Bénoît has rheumatism."

"Poor Bénoît!" said Julie, with a meaning toss of her head.

"Poor Bénoît," responded Annette gently. Her voice was always sweet. One would never have known that Bénoît was a drunken idler.

"Come in. I will give you the meal from my own. Then it will cost you nothing," said Julie, with an air.

"Thank you, Julie, but I would rather pay."

"I do not sell my meal," answered Julie. "What's a few pounds of meal to the wife of Farette? I will get it for you. Come in, Annette."

She turned towards the door, then stopped all at once. There was the oatmeal which she had thrown at Parpon, the basin, and the poker. She wished she had not asked Annette in. But in some things she had a quick wit, and she hurried to say: "It was that yellow cat of Parpon's. It spilt the meal, and I went at it with the poker."

Perhaps Annette believed her. She did not think about it one way or the other; her mind was with the sick Bénoît. She nodded and said nothing, hoping that the flax-seed would be got at once. But when she saw that Julie expected an answer, she said: "Cecilia, my little girl, has a black cat—so handsome. It came from the house of the poor Seigneur de la Rivière a year ago. We took it back, but it would not stay."

Annette spoke simply and frankly, but her words cut like a knife.

Julie responded, with a click of malice: "Look out that the black cat doesn't kill the dear Cecilia."

Annette started, but she did not believe that cats sucked the life from children's lungs, and she replied calmly: "I am not afraid; the good God keeps my child." She then got up and came to Julie, and said: "It is a pity, Julie, that you have not a child. A child makes all right."

Julie was wild to say a fierce thing, for it seemed that Annette was setting off Bénoît against Farette; but the next moment she grew hot, her eyes smarted, and there was a hint of trouble at her throat. She had lived very fast in the last few hours, and it was telling on her. She could not rule herself—she could not play a part so well as she wished. She had not before felt the thing that gave a new pulse to her body and a joyful pain at her breasts. Her eyes got thickly blurred so that she could not see Annette, and, without a word, she hurried to get the meal. She was silent when she came back. She put the meal into Annette's hands. She felt that she would like to talk of Armand. She knew now there was no evil thought in Annette. She did not like her more for that, but she felt she must talk, and Annette was safe. So she took her arm. "Sit down, Annette," she said. "You come so seldom."

"But there is Bénoît, and the child—"

"The child has the black cat from the House!" There was again a sly ring to Julie's voice, and she almost pressed Annette into a chair.

"Well, it must only be a minute."

"Were you at the funeral to-day?" Julie began.

"No; I was nursing Bénoît. But the poor Seigneur! They say he died without confession. No one was there except M'sieu' Medallion, the Little Chemist, Old Sylvie, and M'sieu' Armand. But, of course, you have heard everything."

"Is that all you know?" queried Julie.

"Not much more. I go out little, and no one comes to me except the Little Chemist's wife—she is a good woman."

"What did she say?"

"Only something of the night the Seigneur died. He was sitting in his chair, not afraid, but very sad, we can guess. By-and-by he raised his head quickly. 'I hear a voice in the Tall Porch,' he said. They thought he was dreaming. But he said other things, and cried again that he heard his son's voice in the Porch. They went and found M'sieu' Armand. Then a great supper was got ready, and he sat very grand at the head of the table, but died quickly, when making a grand speech. It was strange he was so happy, for he did not confess—he hadn't absolution."

This was more than Julie had heard. She showed excitement.

"The Seigneur and M'sieu' Armand were good friends when he died?" she asked.

"Quite."

All at once Annette remembered the old talk about Armand and Julie. She was confused. She wished she could get up and run away; but haste would look strange.

"You were at the funeral?" she added, after a minute.

"Everybody was there."

"I suppose M'sieu' Armand looks very fine and strange after his long travel," said Annette shyly, rising to go.

"He was always the grandest gentleman in the province," answered Julie, in her old vain manner. "You should have seen the women look at him to-day! But they are nothing to him—he is not easy to please."

"Good day," said Annette, shocked and sad, moving from the door. Suddenly she turned, and laid a hand on Julie's arm. "Come and see my sweet Cecilia," she said. "She is gay; she will amuse you."

She was thinking again what a pity it was that Julie had no child.

"To see Cecilia and the black cat? Very well—someday."

You could not have told what she meant. But, as Annette turned away again, she glanced at the mill; and there, high up in the dormer window, sat Parpon, his yellow cat on his shoulder, grinning down at her.

She wheeled and went into the house.

II

Parpon sat in the dormer window for a long time, the cat purring against his head, and not seeming the least afraid of falling, though its master was well out on the window-ledge. He kept mumbling to himself:

"Ho, ho, Farette is below there with the gun, rubbing and rubbing at the rust! Holy mother, how it will kick! But he will only meddle. If she set her eye at him and come up bold and said: 'Farette, go and have your whiskey-wine, and then to bed,' he would sneak away. But he has heard something. Some fool, perhaps that Bénoît— no, he is sick—perhaps the herb-woman has been talking, and he thinks he will make a fuss. But it will be nothing. And M'sieu'

Armand, will he look at her?" He chuckled at the cat, which set its head back and hissed in reply. Then he sang something to himself.

Parpon was a poor little dwarf with a big head, but he had one thing which made up for all, though no one knew it—or, at least, he thought so. The Curé himself did not know. He had a beautiful voice. Even in speaking it was pleasant to hear, though he roughened it in a way. It pleased him that he had something of which the finest man or woman would be glad. He had said to himself many times that even Armand de la Rivière would envy him.

Sometimes Parpon went off away into the Bois Noir, and, perched there in a tree, sang away—a man, shaped something like an animal, with a voice like a muffled silver bell.

Some of his songs he had made himself: wild things, broken thoughts, not altogether human; the language of a world between man and the spirits. But it was all pleasant to hear, even when, at times, there ran a weird, dark thread through the woof. No one in the valley had ever heard the thing he sang softly as he sat looking down at Julie:

> "The little white smoke blows there, blows here,
>> The little blue wolf comes down—
>>> *C est la!*
> And the hill-dwarf laughs in the young wife's ear,
>> When the devil comes back to town—
>>> *C est la!*"

It was crooned quietly, but it was distinct and melodious, and the cat purred an accompaniment, its head thrust into his thick black hair. From where Parpon sat he could see the House with the Tall Porch, and, as he sang, his eyes ran from the miller's doorway to it.

Off in the grounds of the dead Seigneur's manor he could see a man push the pebbles with his foot, or twist the branch of a shrub thoughtfully as he walked. At last another man entered the garden. The two greeted warmly, and passed up and down together.

III

"My good friend," said the Curé, "it is too late to mourn for those lost years. Nothing can give them back. As Parpon the dwarf said—you remember him, a wise little man, that Parpon—as he said one day, 'For everything you lose you get something, if only how to laugh at yourself.'"

Armand nodded thoughtfully and answered: "You are right—you and Parpon. But I cannot forgive myself; he was so fine a man: tall, with a grand look, and a tongue like a book. Yes, yes, I can laugh at myself—for a fool."

He thrust his hands into his pockets, and tapped the ground nervously with his foot, shrugging his shoulders a little. The priest took off his hat and made the sacred gesture, his lips moving. Armand caught off his hat also, and said: "You pray—for him?"

"For the peace of a good man's soul."

"He did not confess; he had no rites of the Church; he had refused you many years."

"My son, he had a confessor."

Armand raised his eyebrows. "They told me of no one."

"It was the Angel of Patience."

They walked on again for a time without a word. At last the Curé said: "You will remain here?"

"I cannot tell. This 'here' is a small world, and the little life may fret me. Nor do I know what I have of this,"—he waved his hands towards the house,—"or of my father's property. I may need to be a wanderer again."

"God forbid! Have you not seen the will?"

"I have got no farther than his grave," was the sombre reply.

The priest sighed. They paced the walk again in silence. At last the Curé said: "You will make the place cheerful, as it once was."

"You are persistent," replied the young man, smiling. "Whoever lives here should make it less gloomy."

"We shall soon know who is to live here. See, there is Monsieur Garon, and Monsieur Medallion also."

"The Avocat to tell secrets, the auctioneer to sell them—eh?" Armand went forward to the gate. Like most people, he found Medallion interesting, and the Avocat and he were old friends.

"You did not send for me, monsieur," said the Avocat timidly, "but I thought it well to come, that you might know how things are; and Monsieur Medallion came because he is a witness to the will, and, in a case"—here the little man coughed nervously—"joint executor with Monsieur le Curé."

They entered the house. In a business-like way Armand motioned them to chairs, opened the curtains, and rang the bell. The old housekeeper appeared, a sorrowful joy in her face, and Armand said: "Give us a bottle of the white-top, Sylvie, if there is any left."

"There is plenty, monsieur," she said; "none has been drunk these twelve years."

The Avocat coughed, and said hesitatingly to Armand: "I asked Parpon the dwarf to come, monsieur. There is a reason."

Armand raised his eyebrows in surprise. "Very good," he said. "When will he be here?"

"He is waiting at the Louis Quinze hotel."

"I will send for him," said Armand, and gave the message to Sylvie, who was entering the room.

After they had drunk the wine placed before them, there was silence for a moment, for all were wondering why Parpon should be remembered in the Seigneur's Will.

"Well," said Medallion at last, "a strange little dog is Parpon. I could surprise you about him—and there isn't any reason why I should keep the thing to myself. One day I was up among the rocks, looking for a strayed horse. I got tired, and lay down in the shade of the Rock of Red Pigeons—you know it. I fell asleep. Something waked me. I got up and heard the finest singing you can guess: not like any I ever heard; a wild, beautiful, shivery sort of thing. I listened for a long time. At last it stopped. Then something slid down the rock. I peeped out, and saw Parpon toddling away."

The Curé stared incredulously, the Avocat took off his glasses and tapped his lips musingly, Armand whistled softly.

"So," said Armand at last, "we have the jewel in the toad's head. The clever imp hid it all these years—even from you, Monsieur le Curé."

"Even from me," said the Curé, smiling. Then, gravely: "It is strange, the angel in the stunted body."

"Are you sure it's an angel?" said Armand.

"Who ever knew Parpon do any harm?" queried the Curé.

"He has always been kind to the poor," put in the Avocat.

"With the miller's flour," laughed Medallion: "a pardonable sin."
He sent a quizzical look at the Curé.

"Do you remember the words of Parpon's song?" asked Armand.

"Only a few lines; and those not easy to understand, unless one
had an inkling."

"Had you the inkling?"

"Perhaps, monsieur," replied Medallion seriously.

They eyed each other.

"We will have Parpon in after the will is read," said Armand
suddenly, looking at the Avocat. The Avocat drew the deed from his
pocket. He looked up hesitatingly, and then said to Armand: "You
insist on it being read now?"

Armand nodded coolly, after a quick glance at Medallion. Then
the Avocat began, and read to that point where the Seigneur
bequeathed all his property to his son, should he return—on a
condition. When the Avocat came to the condition Armand stopped
him.

"I do not know in the least what it may be," he said, "but there is
only one by which I could feel bound. I will tell you. My father and I
quarrelled"—here he paused for a moment, clinching his hands
before him on the table—"about a woman; and years of misery came.
I was to blame in not obeying him. I ought not to have given any
cause for gossip. Whatever the condition as to that matter may be, I
will fulfil it. My father is more to me than any woman in the world;
his love of me was greater than that of any woman. I know the
world—and women."

There was a silence. He waved his hand to the Avocat to go on,
and as he did so the Curé caught his arm with a quick, affectionate
gesture. Then Monsieur Garon read the conditions: "That Farette

the miller should have a deed of the land on which his mill was built, with the dam of the mill—provided that Armand should never so much as by a word again address Julie, the miller's wife. If he agreed to the condition, with solemn oath before the Curé, his blessing would rest upon his dear son, whom he still hoped to see before he died."

When the reading ceased there was silence for a moment, then Armand stood up, and took the will from the Avocat; but instantly, without looking at it, handed it back. "The reading is not finished," he said. "And if I do not accept the condition, what then?"

Again Monsieur Garon read, his voice trembling a little. The words of the will ran: "But if this condition be not satisfied, I bequeath to my son Armand the house known as the House with the Tall Porch, and the land, according to the deed thereof; and the residue of my property—with the exception of two thousand dollars, which I leave to the Curé of the parish, the good Monsieur Fabre—I bequeath to Parpon the dwarf."

Then followed a clause providing that, in any case, Parpon should have in fee simple the land known as the Bois Noir, and the hut thereon.

Armand sprang to his feet in surprise, blurting out something, then sat down, quietly took the will, and read it through carefully. When he had finished he looked inquiringly, first at Monsieur Garon, then at the Curé. "Why Parpon?" he said searchingly.

The Curé, amazed, spread out his hands in a helpless way. At that moment Sylvie announced Parpon. Armand asked that he should be sent in. "We'll talk of the will afterwards," he added.

Parpon trotted in, the door closed, and he stood blinking at them. Armand put a stool on the table. "Sit here, Parpon," he said.

Medallion caught the dwarf under the arms and lifted him on the table.

Parpon looked at Armand furtively. "The wild hawk comes back to its nest," he said. "Well, well, what is it you want with the poor Parpon?"

He sat down and dropped his chin in his hands, looking round keenly. Armand nodded to Medallion, and Medallion to the priest, but the priest nodded back again. Then Medallion said: "You and I know the Rock of Red Pigeons, Parpon. It is a good place to perch. One's voice is all to one's self there, as you know. Well, sing us the song of the little brown diver."

Parpon's hands twitched in his beard. He looked fixedly at Medallion. Presently he turned towards the Curé, and shrank so that he looked smaller still.

"It's all right, little son," said the Curé kindly.

Turning sharply on Medallion, Parpon said: "When was it you heard?"

Medallion told him. He nodded, then sat very still. They said nothing, but watched him. They saw his eyes grow distant and absorbed, and his face took on a shining look, so that its ugliness was almost beautiful. All at once he slid from the stool and crouched on his knees. Then he sent out a low long note, like the toll of the bell-bird. From that time no one stirred as he sang, but sat and watched him. They did not even hear Sylvie steal in gently and stand in the curtains at the door.

The song was weird, with a strange thrilling charm; it had the slow dignity of a chant, the roll of an epic, the delight of wild beauty. It told of the little good Folk of the Scarlet Hills, in vague allusive phrases: their noiseless wanderings; their sojourning with the eagle, the wolf, and the deer; their triumph over the winds, the whirlpools, and the spirits of evil fame. It filled the room with the cry of the west wind; it called out of the frozen seas ghosts of forgotten worlds; it coaxed the soft breezes out of the South; it made them all to be at the whistle of the Scarlet Hunter who ruled the North.

Then, passing through veil after veil of mystery, it told of a grand Seigneur whose boat was overturned in a whirlpool, and was saved by a little brown diver. And the end of it all, and the heart of it all, was in the last few lines, clear of allegory:

> "And the wheel goes round in the village mill,
> And the little brown diver he tells the grain. . .
> And the grand Seigneur he has gone to meet
> The little good Folk of the Scarlet Hills!"

At first, all were so impressed by the strange power of Parpon's voice, that they were hardly conscious of the story he was telling. But when he sang of the Seigneur they began to read his parable. Their hearts throbbed painfully.

As the last notes died away Armand got up, and standing by the table, said: "Parpon, you saved my father's life once?"

Parpon did not answer.

"Will you not tell him, my son?" said the Curé, rising. Still Parpon was silent.

"The son of your grand Seigneur asks you a question, Parpon," said Medallion soothingly.

"Oh, my grand Seigneur!" said Parpon, throwing up his hands. "Once he said to me, 'Come, my brown diver, and live with me.' But I said, 'No, I am not fit. I will never go to you at the House with the

Tall Porch.' And I made him promise that he would never tell of it. And so I have lived sometimes with old Farette." Then he laughed strangely again, and sent a furtive look at Armand.

"Parpon," said Armand gently, "our grand Seigneur has left you the Bois Noir for your own. So the hills and the Rock of Red Pigeons are for you—and the little good people, if you like."

Parpon, with fiery eyes, gathered himself up with a quick movement, then broke out: "Oh, my grand Seigneur—my grand Seigneur!" and fell forward, his head in his arms, laughing and sobbing together.

Armand touched his shoulder. "Parpon!" But Parpon shrank away.

Armand turned to the rest. "I do not understand it, gentlemen. Parpon does not like the young Seigneur as he liked the old."

Medallion, sitting in the shadow, smiled. He understood. Armand continued: "As for this 'testament, gentlemen, I will fulfil its conditions; though I swear, were I otherwise minded regarding the woman"—here Parpon raised his head swiftly—"I would not hang my hat for an hour in the Tall Porch."

They rose and shook hands, then the wine was poured out, and they drank it off in silence. Parpon, however, sat with his head in his hands.

"Come, little comrade, drink," said Medallion, offering him a glass.

Parpon made no reply, but caught up the will, kissed it, put it into Armand's hand, and then, jumping down from the table, ran to the door and disappeared through it.

IV

The next afternoon the Avocat visited old Farette. Farette was polishing a gun, mumbling the while. Sitting on some bags of meal was Parpon, with a fierce twinkle in his eye. Monsieur Garon told Farette briefly what the Seigneur had left him. With a quick, greedy chuckle Farette threw the gun away.

"Man alive!" said he; "tell me all about it. Ah, the good news!"

"There is nothing to tell: he left it; that is all."

"Oh, the good Seigneur," cried Farette, "the grand Seigneur!"

Some one laughed scornfully in the doorway. It was Julie.

"Look there," she cried; "he gets the land, and throws away the gun! Brag and coward, miller! It is for *me* to say 'the grand Seigneur!'"

She tossed her head: she thought the old Seigneur had relented towards her. She turned away to the house with a flaunting air, and got her hat. At first she thought she would go to the House with the Tall Porch, but she changed her mind, and went to the Bois Noir instead. Parpon followed her a distance off. Behind, in the mill, Farette was chuckling and rubbing his hands.

Meanwhile, Armand was making his way towards the Bois Noir. All at once, in the shade of a great pine, he stopped. He looked about him astonished.

"This is the old place. What a fool I was, then!" he said.

At that moment Julie came quickly, and lifted her hands towards him. "Armand—beloved Armand!" she said.

Armand looked at her sternly, from her feet to her pitted forehead, then wheeled, and left her without a word.

She sank in a heap on the ground. There was a sudden burst of tears, and then she clinched her hands with fury.

Some one laughed in the trees above her—a shrill, wild laugh. She looked up frightened. Parpon presently dropped down beside her.

"It was as I said," whispered the dwarf, and he touched her shoulder. This was the full cup of shame. She was silent.

"There are others," he whispered again. She could not see his strange smile; but she noticed that his voice was not as usual. "Listen," he urged, and he sang softly over her shoulder for quite a minute. She was amazed.

"Sing again," she said.

"I have wanted to sing to you like that for many years," he replied; and he sang a little more. "He cannot sing like that," he wheedled, and he stretched his arm around her shoulder.

She hung her head, then flung it back again as she thought of Armand.

"I hate him!" she cried; "I hate him!"

"You will not throw meal on me any more, or call me idiot?" he pleaded.

"No, Parpon," she said.

He kissed her on the cheek. She did not resent it. But now he drew away, smiled wickedly at her, and said: "See, we are even now, poor Julie!" Then he laughed, holding his little sides with huge hands. "Imbecile!" he added, and, turning, trotted away towards the Rock of Red Pigeons.

She threw herself, face forward, in the dusty needles of the pines.

When she rose from her humiliation, her face was as one who has seen the rags of harlequinade stripped from that mummer Life,[50]

---

[50] A mummer is a performer in a pantomime; in this metaphor, Julie apprehends the stark reality of existence beneath the surface masquerade of her life.

leaving only naked being. She had touched the limits of the endurable; her sordid little hopes had split into fragments. But when a human soul faces upon its past, and sees a gargoyle at every milestone where an angel should be, and in one flash of illumination—the touch of genius to the smallest mind—understands the pitiless comedy, there comes the still stoic outlook.

Julie was transformed. All the possible years of her life were gathered into the force of one dreadful moment—dreadful and wonderful. Her mean vanity was lost behind the pale sincerity of her face—she was sincere at last. The trivial commonness was gone from her coquetting shoulders and drooping eyelids; and from her body had passed its flexuous softness. She was a woman; suffering, human, paying the price.

She walked slowly the way that Parpon had gone. Looking neither to right nor left, she climbed the long hillside, and at last reached the summit, where, bundled in a steep corner, was the Rock of Red Pigeons. As she emerged from the pines, she stood for a moment, and leaned with outstretched hand against a tree, looking into the sunlight. Slowly her eyes shifted from the Rock to the great ravine, to whose farther side the sun was giving bastions of gold. She was quiet. Presently she stepped into the light and came softly to the Rock. She walked slowly round it as though looking for someone. At the lowest side of the Rock, rude narrow hollows were cut for the feet. With a singular ease she climbed to the top of it. It had a kind of hollow, in which was a rude seat, carved out of the stone. Seeing this, a set look came to her face: she was thinking of Parpon, the master of this place. Her business was with him.

She got down slowly, and came over to the edge of the precipice. Steadying herself against a sapling, she looked over. Down below was a whirlpool, rising and falling—a hungry funnel of death. She drew back. Presently she peered again, and once more withdrew. She gazed round, and then made another tour of the hill, searching. She returned to the precipice. As she did so she heard a voice. She looked and saw Parpon seated upon a ledge of rock not far below. A mocking laugh floated up to her. But there was trouble in the laugh too—a bitter sickness. She did not notice that. She looked about her. Not far away was a stone, too heavy to carry but perhaps not too heavy to roll!

Foot by foot she rolled it over. She looked. He was still there. She stepped back. As she did so a few pebbles crumbled away from her feet and fell where Parpon perched. She did not see or hear them fall. He looked up, and saw the stone creeping upon the edge. Like a flash he was on his feet, and, springing into the air to the right, caught a tree steadfast in the rock. The stone fell upon the ledge, and bounded off again. The look of the woman did not follow the stone. She ran to the spot above the whirlpool, and sprang out and down.

From Parpon there came a wail such as the hills of the north never heard before. Dropping upon a ledge beneath, and from that to a jutting tree, which gave way, he shot down into the whirlpool. He caught Julie's body as it was churned from life to death: and then he fought. There was a demon in the whirlpool, but God and demon were working in the man. Nothing on earth could have unloosed that long, brown arm from Julie's drenched body. The sun lifted an eyelid over the yellow bastions of rock, and saw the fight. Once, twice, the shaggy head was caught beneath the surface—but at last the man conquered.

Inch by inch, foot by foot, Parpon, with the lifeless Julie clamped in one arm, climbed the rough wall, on, on, up to the Rock of Red

Pigeons. He bore her to the top of it. Then he laid her down, and pillowed her head on his wet coat.

The huge hands came slowly down Julie's soaked hair, along her blanched cheek and shoulders, caught her arms and held them. He peered into her face. The eyes had the film which veils Here from Hereafter. On the lips was a mocking smile. He stooped as if to kiss her. The smile stopped him. He drew back for a time, then he leaned forward, shut his eyes, and her cold lips were his.

Twilight—dusk—night came upon Parpon and his dead—the woman whom an impish fate had put into his heart with mockery and futile pain.

TIMES WERE HARD
IN PONTIAC

It was soon after the Rebellion,[51] and there was little food to be had and less money, and winter was at hand. Pontiac, ever most loyal to old France, though obedient to the English, had herself sent few recruits to be shot down by Colborne;[52] but she had emptied her pockets in sending to the front the fulness of her barns and the best cattle of her fields. She gave her all; she was frank in giving, hid nothing; and when her own trouble came there was no voice calling on her behalf. And Pontiac would rather starve than beg. So, as the winter went on, she starved in silence, and no one had more than

---

[51] The 1837 armed conflict between the rebels of Quebec, then Lower Canada, and the British colonial government.

[52] British Army officer John Colborne (1778–1863) became Lieutenant Governor of Upper Canada in August 1828. In 1836 he became commander-in-chief of all the armed forces in British North America. He personally led the offensive at the Battle of Saint-Eustache in December 1837. In this battle the French Canadian "Patriotes" were decisively defeated, with overall losses of 70 dead and 120 prisoners.

sour milk and bread and a potato now and then. The Curé, the Avocat, and the Little Chemist fared no better than the habitants; for they gave all they had right and left, and themselves often went hungry to bed. And the truth is that few outside Pontiac knew of her suffering; she kept the secret of it close.

It seemed at last, however, to the Curé that he must, after all, write to the world outside for help. That was when he saw the faces of the children get pale and drawn. There never was a time when there were so few fish in the river and so little game in the woods. At last, from the altar steps one Sunday, the Curé, with a calm, sad voice, told the people that, for "the dear children's sake," they must sink their pride and ask help from without. He would write first to the Bishop of Quebec; "for," said he, "Mother Church will help us; she will give us food, and money to buy seed in the spring; and, please God, we will pay all back in a year or two!" He paused a minute, then continued: "Some one must go, to speak plainly and wisely of our trouble, that there be no mistake—we are not beggars, we are only borrowers. Who will go? I may not myself, for who would give the Blessed Sacrament, and speak to the sick, or say Mass and comfort you?"

There was silence in the church for a moment, and many faces meanwhile turned instinctively to M. Garon the Avocat, and some to the Little Chemist.

"Who will go?" asked the Curé again. "It is a bitter journey, but our pride must not be our shame in the end. Who will go?"

Every one expected that the Avocat or the Little Chemist would rise; but while they looked at each other, waiting and sorrowful, and the Avocat's fingers fluttered to the seat in front of him, to draw himself up, a voice came from the corner opposite, saying: "M'sieu' le Curé, I will go."

A strange, painful silence fell on the people for a moment, and then went round an almost incredulous whisper: "Parpon the dwarf!"

Parpon's deep eyes were fixed on the Curé, his hunched body leaning on the railing in front of him, his long, strong arms stretched out as if he were begging for some good thing. The murmur among the people increased, but the Curé raised his hand to command silence, and his eyes gazed steadily at the dwarf. It might seem that he was noting the huge head, the shaggy hair, the overhanging brows, the weird face of this distortion of a thing made in God's own image. But he was thinking instead of how the angel and the devil may live side by side in a man, and neither be entirely driven out—and the angel conquer in great times and seasons.

He beckoned to Parpon to come over, and the dwarf trotted with a sidelong motion to the chancel steps. Every face in the congregation was eager, and some were mystified, even anxious. They all knew the singular power of the little man—his knowledge, his deep wit, his judgment, his occasional fierceness, his infrequent malice; but he was kind to children and the sick, and the Curé and the Avocat and their little coterie respected him. Once everybody had worshipped him: that was when he had sung in the Mass, the day of the funeral of the wife of Farette the miller, for whom he worked. It had been rumoured that in his hut by the Rock of Red Pigeons, up at Dalgrothe Mountain, a voice of most wonderful power and sweetness had been heard singing; but this was only rumour. Yet when the body of the miller's wife lay in the church, he had sung so that men and women wept and held each other's hands for joy. He had never sung since, however; his voice of silver was locked away in the cabinet of secret purposes which every man has somewhere in his own soul.

"What will you say to the Bishop, Parpon?" asked the Curé.

The congregation stirred in their seats, for they saw that the Curé intended Parpon to go.

Parpon went up two steps of the chancel quietly and caught the arm of the Curé, drawing him down to whisper in his ear.

A flush and then a peculiar soft light passed over the Curé's face, and he raised his hand over Parpon's head in benediction and said: "Go, my son, and the blessing of God and of His dear Son be with you."

Then suddenly he turned to the altar, and, raising his hands, he tried to speak, but only said: "O Lord, Thou knowest our pride and our vanity, hear us, and—"

Soon afterwards, with tearful eyes, he preached from the text:

'And the Light shineth in darkness, and the darkness comprehendeth it not."

Five days later a little, uncouth man took off his hat in the chief street of Quebec, and began to sing a song of Picardy to an air which no man in French Canada had ever heard. Little farmers on their way to the market by the Place de Cathedral stopped, listening, though every moment's delay lessened their chances of getting a stand in the market-place. Butchers and milkmen loitered, regardless of waiting customers; a little company of soldiers caught up the chorus, and, to avoid involuntary revolt, their sergeant halted them, that they might listen. Gentlemen strolling by—doctor, lawyer, officer, idler—paused and forgot the raw climate, for this marvellous voice in the unshapely body warmed them, and they pushed in among the fast-gathering crowd. Ladies hurrying by in their sleighs lost their hearts to the thrilling notes of:

> "Little grey fisherman,
> Where is your daughter?
> Where is your daughter so sweet?
> Little grey man who comes Over the water,
> I have knelt down at her feet,
> Knelt at your Gabrielle's feet—*ci ci.*"

Presently the wife of the governor stepped out from her sleigh, and, coming over, quickly took Parpon's cap from his hand and went round among the crowd with it, gathering money.

"He is hungry, he is poor," she said, with tears in her eyes. She had known the song in her childhood, and he who used to sing it to her was in her sight no more. In vain the gentlemen would have taken the cap from her; she gathered the money herself, and others followed, and Parpon sang on.

A night later a crowd gathered in the great hall of the city, filling it to the doors, to hear the dwarf sing. He came on the platform dressed as he had entered the city, with heavy, home-made coat and trousers, and moccasins, and a red woollen comforter about his neck—but this comforter he took off when he began to sing. Old France and New France, and the loves and hates and joys and sorrows of all lands, met that night in the soul of this dwarf with the divine voice, who did not give them his name, so that they called him, for want of a better title, the Provençal. And again two nights afterwards it was the same, and yet again a third night and a fourth, and the simple folk, and wise folk also, went mad after Parpon the dwarf.

Then, suddenly, he disappeared from Quebec City, and the next Sunday morning, while the Curé was saying the last words of the Mass, he entered the Church of St. Saviour's at Pontiac. Going up to the chancel steps he waited. The murmuring of the people drew the Curé's attention, and then, seeing Parpon, he came forward.

Parpon drew from his breast a bag, and put it in his hands, and beckoning down the Curé's head, he whispered.

The Curé turned to the altar and raised the bag towards it in ascription and thanksgiving, then he turned to Parpon again, but the dwarf was trotting away down the aisle and from the church.

"Dear children," said the Curé, "we are saved, and we are not shamed." He held up the bag. "Parpon has brought us two thousand dollars: we shall have food to eat, and there shall be more money against seed-time. The giver of this good gift demands that his name be not known. Such is all true charity. Let us pray."

So hard times passed from Pontiac as the months went on; but none save the Curé and the Avocat knew who had helped her in her hour of need.

MEDALLION'S WIIIM

When the Avocat began to lose his health and spirits, and there crept through his shrewd gravity and kindliness a petulance and dejection, Medallion was the only person who had an inspiriting effect upon him. The Little Chemist had decided that the change in him was due to bad circulation and failing powers: which was only partially true.

Medallion made a deeper guess. "Want to know what's the matter with him?" he said. "Ha, I'll tell you! Woman."

"Woman—God bless me!" said the Little Chemist, in a frightened way.

"Woman, little man; I mean the want of a woman," said Medallion.

The Curé, who was present, shrugged his shoulders. "He has an excellent cook, and his bed and jackets are well aired; I see them constantly at the windows."

A laugh gurgled in Medallion's throat. He loved these innocent folk; but himself went twice a year to Quebec City and had more expanded views.

"Woman, Padre"—nodding to the priest, and rubbing his chin so that it rasped like sand-paper—"Woman, my druggist"—throwing a sly look at the Chemist—"woman, neither as cook nor bottle-washer, is what he needs. Every man out of holy orders"—this in deference to his good friend the Curé—"arrives at the time when his youth must be renewed or he becomes as dry bones—like an empty house—furniture sold off. Can only be renewed one way—Woman. Well, here's our Avocat, and there's his remedy. He's got the cooking and the clean fresh linen; he must have a wife, the very best."

"Ah, my friend, you are droll," said the Curé, arching his long fingers at his lips and blowing gently through them, but not smiling in the least; rather serious, almost reproving.

"It is such a whim, such a whim!" said the Little Chemist, shaking his head and looking through his glasses sideways like a wise bird.

"Ha—you shall see! The man must be saved; our Curé shall have his fees; our druggist shall provide the finest essences for the feast—no more pills. And we shall dine with our Avocat once a week—with asparagus in season for the Curé, and a little good wine for all. Ha!"

His *Ha!* was never a laugh; it was unctuous, abrupt, an ejaculation of satisfaction, knowledge, solid enjoyment, final solution.

The Curé shook his head doubtfully; he did not see the need; he did not believe in Medallion's whim; still he knew that the man's judgment was shrewd in most things, and he would be silent and wait. But he shrank from any new phase of life likely to alter the conditions of that old companionship, which included themselves, the Avocat, and the young Doctor, who, like the Little Chemist, was married.

The Chemist sharply said: "Well, well, perhaps. I hope. There is a poetry (his English was not perfect, and at times he mixed it with French in an amusing manner), a little *chanson*, which runs:

> "'Sorrowful is the little house,
> The little house by the winding stream;
> All the laughter has died away
>> Out of the little house.
> But down there come from the lofty hills
> Footsteps and eyes agleam,
> Bringing the laughter of yesterday
>> Into the little house,
> By the winding stream and the hills.
> *Di ron, di ron, di ron, di ron-don.*'"

The Little Chemist blushed faintly at the silence that followed his timid, quaint recital. The Curé looked calm and kind, and drawn away as if in thought; but Medallion presently got up, stooped, and laid his long fingers on the shoulder of the apothecary.

"Exactly, little man," he said; "we've both got the same idea in our heads. I've put it hard fact, you've put it soft sentiment; and it's God's truth either way."

Presently the Curé asked, as if from a great distance, so meditative was his voice: "Who will be the woman, Medallion?"

"I've got one in my eye—the very right one for our Avocat; not here, not out of Pontiac, but from St. Jean in the hills—fulfilling your verses, gentle apothecary. She must bring what is fresh—he must feel that the hills have come to him, she that the valley is hers for the first time. A new world for them both. *Ha!*"

'*Regardez ça!* you are a great man," said the Little Chemist.

There was a strange, inscrutable look in the kind priest's eyes. The Avocat had confessed to him in his time.

Medallion took up his hat.

"Where are you going?" said the Little Chemist.

"To our Avocat, and then to St. Jean."

He opened the door and vanished. The two that were left shook their heads and wondered.

Chuckling softly to himself, Medallion strode away through the lane of white-board houses and the smoke of strong *tabac* from these houses, now and then pulling suddenly up to avoid stumbling over a child, where children are numbered by the dozen to every house. He came at last to a house unlike the others, in that it was of stone and larger. He leaned for a moment over the gate, and looked through a window into a room where the Avocat sat propped up with cushions in a great chair, staring gloomily at two candles burning on the table before him. Medallion watched him for a long time. The Avocat never changed his position; he only stared at the candle, and once or twice his lips moved. A woman came in and put a steaming bowl before him, and laid a pipe and matches beside the bowl. She was a very little, thin old woman, quick and quiet and watchful—his housekeeper. The Avocat took no notice of her. She looked at him several times anxiously, and passed backwards and forwards behind him as a hen moves upon the flank of her brood. All at once she stopped. Her small, white fingers, with their large rheumatic knuckles, lay flat on her lips as she stood for an instant musing; then she trotted lightly to a bureau, got pen and paper and ink, reached down a bunch of keys from the mantel, and came and put them all beside the bowl and the pipe. Still the Avocat did not stir, or show that he recognised her. She went to the door, turned, and looked back, her fingers again at her lips, then slowly sidled out of the room. It was long before the Avocat moved. His eyes had not wavered from the space between the candles. At last, however, he glanced down. His eye caught the bowl, then the pipe. He reached out a slow hand for the pipe, and was taking it up, when his glance fell on the keys and the writing material. He put the pipe down, looked up at the door through which the little old woman had gone, gazed round the room, took up the keys, but soon put them down again with a sigh, and settled back in his chair. Now his gaze alternated between that long lane, sloping into shadow between the candles, and the keys.

Medallion threw a leg over the fence and came in a few steps to the door. He opened it quietly and entered. In the dark he felt his way along the wall to the door of the Avocat's room, opened it, and thrust in his ungainly, whimsical face.

'Ha.' he laughed with quick-winking eyes. "Evening, Garon. Live the Code Napoleon! Pipes for two." A change came slowly over the Avocat. His eyes drew away from that vista between the candles, and the strange distant look faded out of them.

"Great is the Code Napoleon!" he said mechanically. Then, presently: "Ah, my friend, Medallion!"

His first words were the answer to a formula which always passed between them on meeting. As soon as Garon had said them, Medallion's lanky body followed his face, and in a moment he had the Avocat's hand in his, swallowing it, of purpose crushing it, so that Monsieur Garon waked up smartly and gave his visitor a pensive smile. Medallion's cheerful nervous vitality seldom failed to inspire whom he chose to inspire with Something of his own life and cheerfulness. In a few moments both the Avocat and himself were smoking, and the contents of the steaming bowl were divided between them. Medallion talked on many things. The little old housekeeper came in, chirped a soft good-evening, flashed a small thankful smile at Medallion, and, after renewing the bowl and lighting two more tall candles, disappeared. Medallion began with the parish, passed to the law, from the law to Napoleon, from Napoleon to France, and from France to the world, drawing out from the Avocat something of his old vivacity and fire. At last Medallion, seeing that the time was ripe, turned his glass round musingly in his fingers before him and said:

"Bénoît, Annette's husband, died to-day, Garon. You knew him. He went singing—gone in the head, but singing as he used to do before he married—or got drunk! Perhaps his youth came back to him when he was going to die, just for a minute."

The Avocat's eye gazed at Medallion earnestly now, and Medallion went on:

"As good singing as you want to hear. You've heard the words of the song—the river drivers sing it:

> "'What is there like to the cry of the bird
>   That sings in its nest in the lilac tree?
> A voice the sweetest you ever have heard;
>   It is there, it is here, *ci ci!*
> It is there, it is here, it must roam and roam,
>   And wander from shore to shore,
> Till I go forth and bring it home,
>   And enter and close my door

Row along, row along home, *ci ci!*"

When Medallion had finished saying the first verse he waited, but the Avocat said nothing; his eyes were now fastened again on that avenue between the candles leading out into the immortal part of him—his past; he was busy with a life that had once been spent in the fields of Fontainebleau and in the shadow of the Pantheon.

Medallion went on:

> "What is there like to the laughing star,
> Far up from the lilac tree?
> A face that's brighter and finer far;
> It laughs and it shines, ci, ci!
> It laughs and it shines, it must roam and roam,
> And travel from shore to shore,
> Till I go forth and bring it home,
> And house it within my door
> Row along, row along home, ci, ci!"

When Medallion had finished he raised his glass and said: "Garon, I drink to home and woman!"

He waited. The Avocat's eyes drew away from the candles again, and he came to his feet suddenly, swaying slightly as he did so. He caught up a glass and, lifting it, said: "I drink to home and—" a little cold burst of laughter came from him, he threw his head back with something like disdain—"and the Code Napoleon!" he added abruptly.

Then he put the glass down without drinking, wheeled back, and dropped into his chair. Presently he got up, took his keys, went over, opened the bureau, and brought back a well-worn note-book which looked like a diary. He seemed to have forgotten Medallion's presence, but it was not so; he had reached the moment of disclosure which comes to every man, no matter how secretive, when he must tell what is on his mind or die. He opened the book with trembling fingers, took a pen and wrote, at first slowly, while Medallion smoked:

"September 13th.—It is five-and-twenty years ago to-day—*Mon Dieu*, how we danced that night on the flags before the Sorbonne! How gay we were in the Maison Bleu! We were gay and happy— Lulie and I—two rooms and a few francs ahead every week. That night we danced and poured out the light wine, because we were to be married to-morrow. Perhaps there would be a child, if the priest blessed us, she whispered to me as we watched the soft-travelling moon in the gardens of the Luxembourg. Well, we danced. There was an artist with us. I saw him catch Lulie about the waist, and kiss her on the neck. She was angry, but I did not think of that; I was mad with wine. I quarrelled with her, and said to her a shameful thing. Then I rushed away. We were not married the next day; I could not find her. One night, soon after, there was a revolution of students at Mont Parnasse.[53] I was hurt. I remember that she came to me then and nursed me, but when I got well she was gone. Then came the secret word from the Government that I must leave the country or go to prison. I came here. Alas! it is long since we danced before the Sorbonne,[54] and supped at the Maison Bleu. I shall never

---

[53] An area of Paris, France, on the left bank of the river Seine, that is a traditional location for students and artists.

[54] The historical house of the former University of Paris.

see again the gardens of the Luxembourg.[55] Well, that was a mad night five-and-twenty years ago!"

His pen went faster and faster. His eyes lighted up, he seemed quite forgetful of Medallion's presence. When he finished, a fresh change came over him. He gathered his thin fingers in a bunch at his lips, and made an airy salute to the warm space between the candles. He drew himself together with a youthful air, and held his grey head gallantly. Youth and age in him seemed almost grotesquely mingled. Sprightly notes from the song of a cafe chantant hovered on his thin, dry lips. Medallion, amused, yet with a hushed kind of feeling through all his nerves, pushed the Avocat's tumbler till it touched his fingers. The thin fingers twined round it, and once more he came to his feet. He raised the glass. "To—" for a minute he got no further— "To the wedding-eve!" he said, and sipped the hot wine. Presently he pushed the little well-worn book over to Medallion. "I have known you fifteen years—read!" he said. He gave Medallion a meaning look out of his now flashing eyes. Medallion's bony face responded cordially. "Of course," he answered, picked up the book, and read what the Avocat had written. It was on the last page. When he had finished reading, he held the book musingly. His whim had suddenly taken on a new colour. The Avocat, who had been walking up and down the room, with the quick step of a young man, stopped before him, took the book from him, turned to the first page, and handed it back silently. Medallion read:

Quebec, September 13th, 18--. It is one year since. I shall learn to laugh some day.

---

[55] The Jardin du Luxembourg was created beginning in 1612 by the widow of King Henry IV of France, for her new residence, the Luxembourg Palace.

Medallion looked up at him. The old man threw back his head, spread out the last page in the book which he had just written, and said defiantly, as though expecting contradiction to his self-deception—"I have learned."

Then he laughed, but the laugh was dry and hollow and painful. It suddenly passed from his wrinkled lips, and he sat down again; but now with an air as of shy ness and shame. "Let us talk," he said, "of— of the Code Napoleon."

The next morning Medallion visited St. Jean in the hills. Five years before he had sold to a new-comer at St. Jean-Madame Lecyr— the furniture of a little house, and there had sprung up between them a quiet friendship, not the less admiring on Medallion's part because Madame Lecyr was a good friend to the poor and sick. She never tired, when they met, of hearing him talk of the Curé, the Little Chemist, and the Avocat; and in the Avocat she seemed to take the most interest, making countless inquiries—countless when spread over many conversations—upon his life during the time Medallion had known him. He knew also that she came to Pontiac, occasionally, but only in the evening; and once of a moonlight night he had seen her standing before the window of the Avocat's house. Once also he had seen her veiled in the little crowded court-room of Pontiac when an interesting case was being tried, and noticed how she watched Monsieur Garon, standing so very still that she seemed lifeless; and how she stole out as soon as he had done speaking.

Medallion had acute instincts, and was supremely a man of self-counsel. What he thought he kept to him self until there seemed necessity to speak. A few days before the momentous one herebefore described he had called at Madame Lecyr's house, and, in course of conversation, told her that the Avocat's health was breaking; that the day before he had got completely fogged in court over the simplest business, and was quite unlike his old, shrewd, kindly self. By this time he was almost prepared to see her turn pale and her fingers flutter at the knitting-needles she held. She made an excuse to leave the room for a moment. He saw a little book lying near the chair from which she had risen. Perhaps it had dropped from her pocket. He picked it up. It was a book of French songs—Beranger's and others less notable. On the fly-leaf was written: "From Victor to Lulie, September 13th, 18––." Presently she came back to him quite recovered and calm, inquired how the Avocat was cared for, and hoped he would have every comfort and care. Medallion grew on the instant bold. He was now certain that Victor was the Avocat, and Lulie was Madame Lecyr. He said abruptly to her: "Why not come and cheer him up—such old friends as you are?"

At that she rose with a little cry, and stared anxiously at him. He pointed to the book of songs. "Don't be angry—I looked," he said.

She breathed quick and hard, and said nothing, but her fingers laced and interlaced nervously in her lap. "If you were friends why don't you go to him?" he said.

She shook her head mournfully. "We were more than friends, and that is different."

"You were his wife?" said Medallion gently.

"It was different," she replied, flushing. "France is not the same as here. We were to be married, but on the eve of our wedding-day there was an end to it all. Only five years ago I found out he was here."

Then she became silent, and would, or could, speak no more; only, she said at last before he went: "You will not tell him, or any one?"

She need not have asked Medallion. He knew many secrets and kept them; which is not the usual way of good-humoured people.

But now, with the story told by the Avocat himself in his mind, he saw the end of the long romance. He came once more to the house of Madame Lecyr, and being admitted, said to her: "You must come at once with me."

She trembled towards him. "He is worse—he is dying!"

He smiled. "Not dying at all. He needs you; come along. I'll tell you as we go."

But she hung back. Then he told her all he had seen and heard the evening before. Without a word further she prepared to go. On the way he turned to her and said: "You are Madame Lecyr?"

"I am as he left me," she replied timidly, but with a kind of pride, too.

"Don't mistake me," he said. "I thought perhaps you had been married since."

The Avocat sat in his little office, feebly fumbling among his papers, as Medallion entered on him and called to him cheerily: "We are coming to see you to-night, Garon—the Curé, our Little Chemist, and the Seigneur; coming to supper."

The Avocat put out his hand courteously; but he said in a shrinking, pained voice: "No, no, not to-night, Medallion. I would wish no visitors this night—of all."

Medallion stooped over him, and caught him by both arms gently. "We shall see," he said. "It is the anniversary," he whispered.

"Ah, *pardon*," said the Avocat, with a reproving pride, and shrank back as if all his nerves had been laid bare. But Medallion turned, opened the door, went out, and let in a woman, who came forward and timidly raised her veil.

"Victor!" Medallion heard, then "Lulie!" and then he shut the door, and, with supper in his mind, went into the kitchen to see the housekeeper, who, in this new joy, had her own tragedy—humming to himself:

> "But down there come from the lofty hills
> Footsteps and eyes agleam,
> Bringing the laughter of yesterday
> Into the little house."

THE PRISONER

His chief occupation in the daytime was to stand on the bench by the small barred window and watch the pigeons on the roof and in the eaves of the house opposite. For five years he had done this. In the summer a great fire seemed to burn beneath the tin of the roof, for a quivering hot air rose from them, and the pigeons never alighted on them, save in the early morning or in the evening. Just over the peak could be seen the topmost branch of a maple, too slight to bear the weight of the pigeons, but the eaves were dark and cool, and there his eyes rested when he tired of the hard blue sky and the glare of the slates.

In winter the roof was covered for weeks and months by a blanket of snow which looked like a shawl of impacted wool, white and restful, and the windows of the house were spread with frost. But the pigeons were always gay, walking on the ledges or crowding on the shelves of the lead pipes. He studied them much, but he loved them more. His prison was less a prison because of them, and during those long five years he found himself more in touch with them than with the wardens of the prison or with any of his fellow-prisoners. To the former he was respectful, and he gave them no trouble at all;

222

with the latter he had nothing in common, for they were criminals, and he—so wild and mad with drink and anger was he at the time, that he had no remembrance, absolutely none, of how Jean Gamache lost his life.

He remembered that they had played cards far into the night; that they had quarrelled, then made their peace; that the others had left; that they had begun gaming and drinking and quarrelling again—and then everything was blurred, save for a vague recollection that he had won all Gamache's money and had pocketed it. Afterwards came a blank.

He waked to find two officers of the law beside him, and the body of Jean Gamache, stark and dreadful, a few feet away.

When the officers put their hands upon him he shook them off; when they did it again he would have fought them to the death, had it not been for his friend, tall Medallion the auctioneer, who laid a strong hand on his arm and said, "Steady, Turgeon, steady!" and he had yielded to the firm friendly pressure.

Medallion had left no stone unturned to clear him at the trial, had himself played detective unceasingly. But the hard facts remained, and on a chain of circumstantial evidence Blaze Turgeon was convicted of manslaughter and sent to prison for ten years. Blaze himself had said that he did not remember, but he could not believe that he had committed the crime. Robbery? He shrugged his shoulders at that, he insisted that his lawyer should not reply to the foolish and insulting suggestion. But the evidence went to show that Gamache had all the winnings when the other members of the party retired, and this very money had been found in Blaze's pocket. There was only Blaze's word that they had played cards again. Anger? Possibly. Blaze could not recall, though he knew they had quarrelled.

The judge himself, charging the jury, said that he never before had seen a prisoner so frank, so outwardly honest, but he warned them that they must not lose sight of the crime itself, the taking of a human life, whereby a woman was made a widow and a child fatherless. The jury found him guilty.

With few remarks the judge delivered his sentence, and then himself, shaken and pale, left the court-room hurriedly, for Blaze Turgeon's father had been his friend from boyhood.

Blaze took his sentence calmly, looking the jury squarely in the eyes, and when the judge stopped, he bowed to him, and then turned to the jury and said:

"Gentlemen, you have ruined my life. You don't know, and I don't know, who killed the man. You have guessed, and I take the penalty. Suppose I'm innocent—how will you feel when the truth comes out? You've known me more or less these twenty years, and you've said, with evidently no more knowledge than I've got, that I did this horrible thing. I don't know but that one of you did it. But you are safe, and I take my ten years!"

He turned from them, and, as he did so, he saw a woman looking at him from a corner of the court-room, with a strange, wild expression. At the moment he saw no more than an excited, bewildered face, but afterwards this face came and went before him, flashing in and out of dark places in a kind of mockery.

As he went from the court-room another woman made her way to him in spite of the guards. It was the Little Chemist's wife, who, years before, had been his father's housekeeper, who knew him when his eyes first opened on the world.

"My poor Blaze! my poor Blaze!" she said, clasping his manacled hands.

*****

In prison he refused to see all visitors, even Medallion, the Little Chemist's wife, and the good Father Fabre. Letters, too, he refused to accept and read. He had no contact, wished no contact with the outer world, but lived his hard, lonely life by himself, silent, studious—for now books were a pleasure to him. He had entered his prison a wild, excitable, dissipated youth, and he had become a mature brooding man. Five years had done the work of twenty.

The face of the woman who looked at him so strangely in the court-room haunted him so that at last it became a part of his real life, lived largely at the window where he looked out at the pigeons on the roof of the hospital.

"She was sorry for me," he said many a time to himself. He was shaken with misery often, so that he rocked to and fro as he sat on his bed, and a warder heard him cry out even in the last days of his imprisonment:

"O God, canst Thou do everything but speak!" And again: "That hour—the memory of that hour, in exchange for my ruined life!"

One day the gaoler came to him and said: "Monsieur Turgeon, you are free. The Governor has cut off five years from your sentence."

Then he was told that people were waiting without—Medallion, the Little Chemist and his wife, and others more important. But he would not go to meet them, and he stepped into the open world alone at dawn the next morning, and looked out upon a still sleeping village. Suddenly there stood before him a woman, who had watched by the prison gates all night; and she put out her hand in entreaty, and said with a breaking voice: "You are free at last!"

He remembered her—the woman who had looked at him so anxiously and sorrowfully in the court-room. "Why did you come to meet me?" he asked.

"I was sorry for you."

"But that is no reason."

"I once committed a crime," she whispered, with shrinking bitterness.

"That's bad," he said. "Were you punished?" He looked at her keenly, almost fiercely, for a curious suspicion shot into his mind.

She shook her head and answered no.

"That's worse!"

"I let some one else take my crime upon him and be punished for it," she said, an agony in her eyes.

"Why was that?"

"I had a little child," was her reply.

"And the man who was punished instead?"

"He was alone in the world," she said.

A bitter smile crept to his lips, and his face was afire. He shut his eyes, and when they opened again discovery was in them.

"I remember you now," he said. "I remember now. I waked and saw you looking at me *that night!* Who was the father of your child?"

"Jean Gamache," she replied. "He ruined me and left me to starve."

"I am innocent of his death!" he said quietly and gladly.

She nodded. He was silent for a moment. "The child still lives?" he asked. She nodded again. "Well, let it be so," he said. "But you owe me five years—and a good name."

"I wish to God I could give them back!" she cried, tears streaming down her cheeks. "It was for my child; he was so young."

"It can't be helped now," he said sighing, and he turned away from her.

"Won't you forgive me?" she asked bitterly.

"Won't you give me back those five years?"

"If the child did not need me I would give my life," she answered. "I owe it to you."

Her haggard, hunted face made him sorry; he, too, had suffered.

"It's all right," he answered gently. "Take care of your child."

Again he moved away from her, and went down the little hill, with a cloud gone from his face that had rested there five years. Once he turned to look back. The woman was gone, but over the prison a flock of pigeons were flying. He took off his hat to them.

Then he went through the town, looking neither to right nor left, and came to his own house, where the summer morning was already entering the open windows, though he had thought to find the place closed and dark.

The Little Chemist's wife met him in the doorway. She could not speak, nor could he, but he kissed her as he had done when he went condemned to prison. Then he passed on to his own room, and entering, sat down before the open window, and peacefully drank in the glory of a new world. But more than once he choked down a sob rising in his throat.

AN UPSET PRICE

Once Secord was as fine a man to look at as you would care to see: with a large intelligent eye, a clear, healthy skin, and a full, brown beard. He walked with a spring, had a gift of conversation, and took life as he found it, never too seriously, yet never carelessly. That was before he left the village of Pontiac in Quebec to offer himself as a surgeon to the American Army. When he came back there was a change in him. He was still handsome, but something of the spring had gone from his walk, the quick light of his eyes had given place to a dark, dreamy expression, his skin became a little dulled, and his talk slower, though not less musical or pleasant. Indeed, his conversation had distinctly improved. Previously there was an undercurrent of self-consciousness; it was all gone now. He talked as one knowing his audience. His office became again, as it had been before, a rendezvous for the few interesting men of the place, including the Avocat, the Curé, the Little Chemist, and Medallion. They played chess and écarté for certain hours of certain evenings in the week at Secord's house.

Medallion was the first to notice that the wife—whom Secord had married soon after he came back from the war—occasionally put down her work and looked with a curious inquiring expression at her husband as he talked. It struck Medallion that she was puzzled by some change in Secord.

Secord was a brilliant surgeon and physician. With the knife or beside a sick-bed, he was admirable. His intuitive perception, so necessary in his work, was very fine: he appeared to get at the core of a patient's trouble, and to decide upon necessary action with instant and absolute confidence. Some delicate operation performed by him was recorded and praised in the *Lancet*;[56] and he was offered a responsible post in a medical college, and, at the same time, the good-will of a valuable practice. He declined both, to the lasting astonishment, yet personal joy, of the Curé and the Avocat; but, as time went on, not so much to the surprise of the Little Chemist and Medallion. After three years, the sleepy Little Chemist waked up suddenly in his chair one day, and said: "*Parbleu*, God bless me!" (he loved to mix his native language with English) got up and went over to Secord's office, adjusted his glasses, looked at Secord closely, caught his hand with both of his own, shook it with shy abruptness, came back to his shop, sat down, and said: "God bless my soul! *Regardez ça!*"

Medallion made his discovery sooner. Watching closely he had seen a pronounced deliberation infused through all Secord's indolence of manner, and noticed that often, before doing anything, the big eyes debated steadfastly, and the long, slender fingers ran down the beard softly. At times there was a deep meditativeness in

---

[56] Founded in 1823, *The Lancet* is one of the world's oldest and best known general medical journals.

the eye, again a dusky fire. But there was a certain charm through it all—a languid precision, a slumbering look in the face, a vague undercurrent in the voice, a fantastical flavour to the thought. The change had come so gradually that only Medallion and the wife had a real conception of how great it was. Medallion had studied Secord from every stand-point. At the very first he wondered if there was a woman in it. Much thinking on a woman, whose influence on his life was evil or disturbing, might account somewhat for the change in Secord. But, seeing how fond the man was of his wife, Medallion gave up that idea. It was not liquor, for Secord never touched it. One day, however, when Medallion was selling the furniture of a house, he put up a feather bed, and, as was his custom—for he was a whimsical fellow—let his humour have play. He used many metaphors as to the virtue of the bed, crowning them with the statement that you slept in it dreaming as delicious dreams as though you had eaten poppy, or mandragora,[57] or—He stopped short, said, "By jingo, that's it!" knocked the bed down instantly, and was an utter failure for the rest of the day.

The wife was longer in discovering the truth, but a certain morning, as her husband lay sleeping after an all-night sitting with a patient, she saw lying beside him—it had dropped from his waistcoat pocket—a little bottle full of a dark liquid. She knew that he always carried his medicine-phials in a pocket-case. She got the case, and saw that none was missing. She noticed that the cork of the phial was well worn. She took it out and smelled the liquid. Then she understood. She waited and watched. She saw him after he waked look watchfully round, quietly take a wine-glass, and let the liquid

[57] One species of poppy is the source of the crude drug opium that contains powerful medicinal alkaloids such as morphine; sometimes known as mandrake, mandragora belongs to the nightshade family and contains hallucinogenic compounds.

come drop by drop into it from the point of his forefinger. Henceforth she read with understanding the changes in his manner, and saw behind the mingled abstraction and fanciful meditation of his talk.

She had not yet made up her mind what to do. She saw that he hid it from her assiduously. He did so more because he wished not to pain her than from furtiveness. By nature he was open and brave, and had always had a reputation for plainness and sincerity. She was in no sense his equal in intelligence or judgment, nor even in instinct. She was a woman of more impulse and constitutional good-nature than depth. It is probable that he knew that, and refrained from letting her into the knowledge of this vice, contracted in the war when, seriously ill, he was able to drag himself about from patient to patient only by the help of opium. He was alive to his position and its consequences, and faced it. He had no children, and he was glad of this for one reason. He could do nothing now without the drug; it was as necessary as light to him. The little bottle had been his friend so long, that, with his finger on its smooth-edged cork, it was as though he held the tap of life.

The Little Chemist and Medallion kept the thing to themselves, but they understood each other in the matter, and wondered what they could do to cure him. The Little Chemist only shrank back, and said, "No, no, *pardon*, my friend!" when Medallion suggested that he should speak to Secord. But the Little Chemist was greatly concerned—for had not Secord saved his beloved wife by a clever operation? and was it not her custom to devote a certain hour every week to the welfare of Secord's soul and body, before the shrine of the Virgin? Her husband told her now that Secord was in trouble, and though he was far from being devout himself, he had a shy faith in the great sincerity of his wife. She did her best, and increased her offerings of flowers to the shrine; also, in her simplicity, she sent Secord's wife little jars of jam to comfort him.

One evening the little *coterie* met by arrangement at the doctor's house. After waiting an hour or two for Secord, who had been called away to a critical case, the Avocat and the Curé went home, leaving polite old-fashioned messages for their absent host; but the Little Chemist and Medallion remained. For a time Mrs. Secord remained with them, then retired, begging them to await her husband, who, she knew, would be grateful if they stayed. The Little Chemist, with timid courtesy, showed her out of the room, then came back and sat down. They were very silent. The Little Chemist took off his glasses a half-dozen times, wiped them, and put them back. Then suddenly turned on Medallion. "You mean to speak to-night?"

"Yes, that's it."

'*Regardez ça*—well, well!"

Medallion never smoked harder than he did then. The Little Chemist looked at him nervously again and again, listened towards the door, fingered with his tumbler, and at last hearing the sound of sleigh-bells, suddenly came to his feet, and said: "*Voilà*, I will go to my wife." And catching up his cap, and forgetting his overcoat, he trotted away home in a fright.

What Medallion did or said to Secord that night neither ever told. But it must have been a singular scene, for when the humourist pleads or prays there is no pathos like it; and certainly Medallion's eyes were red when he rapped up the Little Chemist at dawn, caught him by the shoulders, turned him round several times, thumped him on the back, and called him a bully old boy; and then, seeing the old wife in her quaint padded night-gown, suddenly hugged her, threw himself into a chair, and almost shouted for a cup of coffee.

At the same time Mrs. Secord was alternately crying and laughing in her husband's arms, and he was saying to her: "I'll make a fight for it, Lesley, a big fight; but you must be patient, for I expect I'll be a devil sometimes without it. Why, I've eaten a drachm[58] a day of the stuff, or drunk its equivalent in the tincture. No, never mind praying; be a brick and fight with me that's the game, my girl."

He did make a fight for it, such an one as few men have made and come out safely. For those who dwell in the Pit never suffer as do they who struggle with this appetite. He was too wise to give it up all at once. He diminished the dose gradually, but still very perceptibly. As it was, it made a marked change in him. The necessary effort of the will gave a kind of hard coldness to his face, and he used to walk his garden for hours at night in conflict with his enemy. His nerves were uncertain, but, strange to say, when (it was not often) any serious case of illness came under his hands, he was somehow able to pull himself together and do his task gallantly enough. But he had had no important surgical case since he began his cure. In his heart he lived in fear of one; for he was not quite sure of himself. In spite of effort to the contrary he became irritable, and his old pleasant fantasies changed to gloomy and bizarre imaginings.

The wife never knew what it cost her husband thus, day by day, to take a foe by the throat and hold him in check. She did not guess that he knew if he dropped back even once he could not regain himself: this was his idiosyncrasy. He did not find her a great help to him in his trouble. She was affectionate, but she had not much penetration even where he was concerned, and she did not grasp

---

[58] A tradition British measure (liquid or dry) equal to roughly 3/4 teaspoon.

how much was at stake. She thought indeed that he should be able to give it up all at once. He was tender with her, but he wished often that she could understand him without explanation on his part. Many a time he took out the little bottle with a reckless hand, but conquered himself. He got most help, perhaps, from the honest, cheerful eye of Medallion and the stumbling timorous affection of the Little Chemist. They were perfectly disinterested friends—his wife at times made him aware that he had done her a wrong, for he had married her with this appetite on him. He did not defend himself, but he wished she would—even if she had to act it—make him believe in himself more. One morning against his will he was irritable with her, and she said something that burnt like caustic. He smiled ironically, and pushed his newspaper over to her, pointing to a paragraph. It was the announcement that an old admirer of hers whom she had passed by for her husband, had come into a fortune. "Perhaps you've made a mistake," he said.

She answered nothing, but the look she gave was unfortunate for both. He muffled his mouth in his long silken beard as if to smother what he felt impelled to say, then suddenly rose and left the table.

At this time he had reduced his dose of the drug to eight drops twice a day. With a grim courage he resolved to make it five all at once. He did so, and held to it. Medallion was much with him in these days. One morning in the spring he got up, went out in his garden, drew in the fresh, sweet air with a great gulp, picked some lovely crab-apple blossoms, and, with a strange glowing look in his eyes, came in to his wife, put them into her hands, and kissed her. It was the anniversary of their wedding-day. Then, without a word, he took from his pocket the little phial that he had carried so long, rolled it for an instant in his palm, felt its worn, discoloured cork musingly, and threw it out of the window.

"Now, my dear," he whispered, "we will be happy again."

He held to his determination with a stern anxiety. He took a month's vacation, and came back better. He was not so happy as he hoped to be; yet he would not whisper to himself the reason why. He felt that something had failed him somewhere.

One day a man came riding swiftly up to his door to say that his wife's father had met with a bad accident in his great mill. Secord told his wife. A peculiar troubled look came into his face as he glanced carefully over his instruments and through his medicine case. "God, I must do it alone!" he said.

The old man's injury was a dangerous one: a skilful operation was necessary. As Secord stood beside the sufferer, he felt his nerves suddenly go—just as they did in the war before he first took the drug. His wife was in the next room—he could hear her; he wished she would make no sound at all. Unless this operation was performed successfully the sufferer would die—he might die anyhow. Secord tried to gather himself up to his task, but he felt it was of no use. A month later when he was more recovered physically he would be able to perform the operation, but the old man was dying now, while he stood helplessly stroking his big brown beard. He took up his pocket medicine-case, and went out where his wife was.

Excited and tearful, she started up to meet him, painfully inquiring. "Can you save him?" she said. "Oh, James, what is the matter? You are trembling."

"It's just this way, Lesley: my nerve is broken; I can't perform the operation as I am, and he will die in an hour if I don't."

She caught him by the arm. "Can you not be strong? You have a will. Will you not try to save my father, James? Is there no way?"

"Yes, there is one way," he said. He opened the pocket-case and took out a phial of laudanum.[59] "This is the way. I can pull myself together with it. It will save his life." There was a dogged look in his face.

"Well? well?" she said. "Oh, my dear father, will you not keep him here?"

A peculiar cold smile hovered about his lips. "But there is danger to me in this . . . and remember, he is very old!"

"Oh," she cried, "how can you be so shocking, so cruel!" She rocked herself to and fro. "If it will save him—and you need not take it again, ever!"

"But, I tell you—"

"Do you not hear him—he is dying!" She was mad with grief; she hardly knew what she said.

Without a word he dropped the tincture swiftly in a wine-glass of water, drank it off, shivered, drew himself up with a start, gave a sigh as if some huge struggle was over, and went in to where the old man was. Three hours after he told his wife that her father was safe.

When, after a hasty kiss, she left him and went into the room of sickness, and the door closed after her, standing where she had left him he laughed a hard crackling laugh, and said between his teeth:

"An upset price!"

Then he poured out another portion of the dark tincture—the largest he had ever taken—and tossed it off. That night he might have been seen feeling about the grass in a moon-lit garden. At last

---

[59] A tincture (or solution) of opium, typically containing 10 percent opium.

he put something in his pocket with a quick, harsh chuckle of satisfaction. It was a little black bottle with a well-worn cork.

A FRAGMENT OF LIVES

They met at last, Dubarre, and Villiard, the man who had stolen from him the woman he loved. Both had wronged the woman, but Villiard most, for he had let her die because of jealousy.

They were now in a room alone in the forest of St. Sebastian. Both were quiet, and both knew that the end of their feud was near.

Going to a cupboard Dubarre brought out four glasses and put them on the table. Then from two bottles he poured out what looked like red wine, two glasses from each bottle. Putting the bottles back he returned to the table.

"Do you dare to drink with me?" Dubarre asked, nodding towards the glasses. "Two of the glasses have poison in them, two have good red wine only. We will move them about and then drink. Both may die, or only one of us."

Villiard looked at the other with contracting, questioning eyes.

"You would play that game with me?" he asked, in a mechanical voice.

"It would give me great pleasure." The voice had a strange, ironical tone. "It is a grand sport—as one would take a run at a crevasse and clear it, or fall. If we both fall, we are in good company; if you fall, I have the greater joy of escape; if I fall, you have the same joy."

"I am ready," was the answer. "But let us eat first."

A great fire burned in the chimney, for the night was cool. It filled the room with a gracious heat and with huge, comfortable shadows. Here and there on the wall a tin cup flashed back the radiance of the fire, the barrel of a gun glistened soberly along a rafter, and the long, wiry hair of an otter-skin in the corner sent out little needles of light. Upon the fire a pot was simmering, and a good savour came from it. A wind went lilting by outside the hut in tune with the singing of the kettle. The ticking of a huge, old-fashioned repeating-watch on the wall was in unison with these.

Dubarre rose from the table, threw himself upon the little pile of otter-skins, and lay watching Villiard and mechanically studying the little room.

Villiard took the four glasses filled with the wine and laid them on a shelf against the wall, then began to put the table in order for their supper, and to take the pot from the fire.

Dubarre noticed that just above where the glasses stood on the shelf a crucifix was hanging, and that red crystal sparkled in the hands and feet where the nails should be driven in. There was a painful humour in the association. He smiled, then turned his head away, for old memories flashed through his brain—he had been an acolyte once; he had served at the altar.

Suddenly Dubarre rose, took the glasses from the shelf and placed them in the middle of the table—the death's head for the feast.[60]

As they sat down to eat, the eyes of both men unconsciously wandered to the crucifix, attracted by the red sparkle of the rubies. They drank water with the well-cooked meat of the wapiti,[61] though red wine faced them on the table. Each ate heartily; as though a long day were before them and not the shadow of the Long Night. There was no speech save that of the usual courtesies of the table. The fire, and the wind, and the watch seemed the only living things besides themselves, perched there between heaven and earth.

At length the meal was finished, and the two turned in their chairs towards the fire. There was no other light in the room, and on the faces of the two, still and cold, the flame played idly.

"When?" said Dubarre at last.

"Not yet," was the quiet reply.

"I was thinking of my first theft—an apple from my brother's plate," said Dubarre, with a dry smile. "You?"

"I, of my first lie."

"That apple was the sweetest fruit I ever tasted."

"And I took the penalty of the lie, but I had no sorrow."

Again there was silence.

"Now?" asked Villiard, after an hour had passed.

"I am ready."

They came to the table.

"Shall we bind our eyes?" asked Dubarre. "I do not know the glasses that hold the poison."

---

[60] A death's head is a human skull, a traditional personification of death.
[61] Elk.

"Nor I the bottle that held it. I will turn my back, and do you change about the glasses."

Villiard turned his face towards the timepiece on the wall. As he did so it began to strike—a clear, silvery chime: "One! two! three—!"

Before it had finished striking both men were facing the glasses again.

"Take one," said Dubarre.

Villiard took the one nearest himself. Dubarre took one also. Without a word they lifted the glasses and drank.

"Again," said Dubarre.

"You choose," responded Villiard.

Dubarre lifted the one nearest himself, and Villiard picked up the other. Raising their glasses again, they bowed to each other and drank.

The watch struck twelve, and stopped its silvery chiming.

They both sat down, looking at each other, the light of an enormous chance in their eyes, the tragedy of a great stake in their clinched hands; but the deeper, intenser power was in the face of Dubarre, the explorer.

There was more than power; malice drew down the brows and curled the sensitive upper lip. Each man watched the other for knowledge of his own fate. The glasses lay straggling along the table, emptied of death and life.

All at once a horrible pallor spread over the face of Villiard, and his head jerked forward. He grasped the table with both hands, twitching and trembling. His eyes stared wildly at Dubarre, to whose face the flush of wine had come, whose look was now maliciously triumphant.

Villiard had drunk both glasses of the poison!

"I win!" Dubarre stood up. Then, leaning over the table towards the dying man, he added: "You let her die—well! Would you know the truth? She loved you—always."

Villiard gasped, and his look wandered vaguely along the opposite wall.

Dubarre went on. "I played the game with you honestly, because—because it was the greatest man could play. And I, too, sinned against her. Now die! She loved you—murderer!"

The man's look still wandered distractedly along the wall. The sweat of death was on his face; his lips were moving spasmodically.

Suddenly his look became fixed; he found voice.

'Pardon—Jesu!" he said, and stiffened where he sat.

His eyes were fixed on the jewelled crucifix. Dubarre snatched it from the wall, and hastening to him held it to his lips: but the warm sparkle of the rubies fell on eyes that were cold as frosted glass. Dubarre saw that he was dead.

"Because the woman loved him!" he said, gazing curiously at the dead man.

He turned, went to the door and opened it, for his breath choked him.

All was still on the wooded heights and in the wide valley.

"Because the woman loved him he repented," said Dubarre again with a half-cynical gentleness as he placed the crucifix on the dead man's breast.

THE MAN THAT DIED
AT ALMA

The man who died at Alma had a Kilkenny brogue[62] that you could not cut with a knife, but he was called Kilquhanity, a name as Scotch as McGregor. Kilquhanity was a retired soldier, on pension, and Pontiac was a place of peace and poverty. The only gentry were the Curé, the Avocat, and the young Seigneur, but of the three the only one with a private income was the young Seigneur.

What should such a common man as Kilquhanity do with a private income! It seemed almost suspicious, instead of creditable, to the minds of the simple folk at Pontiac; for they were French, and poor, and laborious, and Kilquhanity drew his pension from the headquarters of the English Government, which they only knew by legends wafted to them over great tracts of country from the city of Quebec.

---

[62] Strong accent from Kilkenny, a city in south-east Ireland.

When Kilquhanity first came with his wife, it was without introductions from anywhere—unlike everybody else in Pontiac, whose family history could be instantly reduced to an exact record by the Curé. He had a smattering of French, which he turned off with oily brusqueness; he was not close-mouthed, he talked freely of events in his past life; and he told some really wonderful tales of his experiences in the British army. He was no braggart, however, and his one great story which gave him the nickname by which he was called at Pontiac, was told far more in a spirit of laughter at himself than in praise of his own part in the incident.

The first time he told the story was in the house of Medallion the auctioneer.

"Aw the night it was," said Kilquhanity, after a pause, blowing a cloud of tobacco smoke into the air, "the night it was, me darlin's! Bitther cowld in that Roosian counthry, though but late summer, and nothin' to ate but a lump of bread, no bigger than a dickybird's skull; nothin' to drink but wather. Turrible, turrible, and for clothes to wear—Mother of Moses! that was a bad day for clothes! We got betune no barrick quilts that night. No stockin' had I insoide me boots, no shirt had I but a harse's quilt sewed an to me; no heart I had insoide me body; nothin' at all but duty an' shtandin' to orders, me b'ys!

"Says Sergeant-Major Kilpatrick to me, 'Kilquhanity,' says he, 'there's betther places than River Alma to live by,' says he. 'Faith, an' by the Liffey I wish I was this moment'—Liffey's in ould Ireland, Frenchies! 'But, Kilquhanity,' says he, 'faith, an' it's the Liffey we'll never see again, an' put that in yer pipe an' smoke it!' And thrue for him.

"But that night, aw that night! Ivery bone in me body was achin', and shure me heart was achin' too, for the poor b'ys that were fightin' hard an' gettin' little for it. Bitther cowld it was, aw, bitther cowld, and the b'ys droppin' down, droppin', droppin', droppin', wid the Roosian bullets in thim!

" 'Kilquhanity,' says Sergeant-Major Kilpatrick to me, 'it's this shtandin' still, while we do be droppin', droppin', that girds the soul av yer.' Aw, the sight it was, the sight it was! The b'ys of the rigimint shtandin' shoulder to shoulder, an' the faces av 'm blue wid powder, an' red wid blood, an' the bits o' b'ys droppin' round me loike twigs of an' ould tree in a shtorm. Just a cry an' a bit av a gurgle tru the teeth, an' divil the wan o' thim would see the Liffey side anny more.

" 'The Roosians are chargin'!' shouts Sergeant-Major Kilpatrick. 'The Roosians are chargin'—here they come!' Shtandin' besoide me was a bit of a lump of a b'y, as foine a lad as ever shtood in the boots of me rigimint—aw! the look of his face was the look o' the dead. 'The Roosians are comin'—they're chargin'!' says Sergeant-Major Kilpatrick, and the bit av a b'y, that had nothin' to eat all day, throws down his gun and turns round to run. Eighteen years old he was, only eighteen—just a straight slip of a lad from Malahide. 'Hould on! Teddie,' says I, 'hould on! How'll yer face yer mother if yer turn yer back on the inimy of yer counthry?' The b'y looks me in the eyes long enough to wink three times, picks up his gun, an' shtood loike a rock, he did, till the Roosians charged us, roared on us, an' I saw me slip of a b'y go down under the sabre of a damned Cossack. 'Mother!' I heard him say, 'Mother!' an' that's all I heard him say—and the mother waitin' away aff there by the Liffey soide. Aw, wurra, wurra, the b'ys go down to battle and the mothers wait at home! Some of the b'ys come back, but the most of thim shtay where the battle laves 'em. Wurra, wurra, many's the b'y wint down that day by Alma River, an' niver come back!

"There I was shtandin', when hell broke loose on the b'ys of me rigimint, and divil the wan o' me knows if I killed a Roosian that day or not. But Sergeant-Major Kilpatrick—a bit of a liar was the Sergeant-Major—says he: 'It was tin ye killed, Kilquhanity.' He says that to me the noight that I left the rigimint for ever, and all the b'ys shtandin' round and liftin' lasses an' saying, 'Kilquhanity! Kilquhanity! Kilquhanity!' as if it was sugar and honey in their mouths. Aw, the sound of it! 'Kilquhanity,' says he, 'it was tin ye killed'; but aw, b'ys, the Sergeant-Major was an awful liar. If he could be doin' annybody anny good by lyin', shure he would be lyin' all the time.

"But it's little I know how many I killed, for I was killed meself that day. A Roosian sabre claved the shoulder and neck of me, an' down I wint, and over me trampled a squadron of Roosian harses, an' I stopped thinkin'. Aw, so aisy, so aisy, I slipped away out av the fight! The shriekin' and roarin' kept dwindlin' and dwindlin', and I dropped all into a foine shlape, so quiet, so aisy. An' I thought that slip av a lad from the Liffey soide was houlding me hand, and sayin' 'Mother! Mother!' and we both wint ashlape; an' the b'ys of the rigimint when Alma was over, they said to each other, the b'ys they said: 'Kilquhanity's dead.' An' the trinches was dug, an' all we foine dead b'ys was laid in long rows loike candles in the trinches. An' I was laid in among thim, and Sergeant-Major Kilpatrick shtandin' there an' looking at me an' sayin': 'Poor b'y—poor b'y!'

"But when they threw another man on tap of me, I waked up out o' that beautiful shlape, and give him a kick. 'Yer not polite,' says I to mesilf. Shure, I couldn't shpake—there was no strength in me. An' they threw another man on, an' I kicked again, and the Sergeant-Major he sees it, an' shouts out. 'Kilquhan ity's leg is kickin'!' says he. An' they pulled aff the two poor divils that had been thrown o' tap o' me, and the Sergeant-Major lifts me head, an' he says 'Yer not killed, Kilquhanity?' says he.

"Divil a word could I shpake, but I winked at him, and Captain Masham shtandin' by whips out a flask.

"'Put that betune his teeth,' says he. Whin I got it there, trust me fur not lettin' it go. An' the Sergeant-Major says to me: 'I have hopes of you, Kilquhanity, when you do be drinkin' loike that.'

"'A foine healthy corpse I am; an' a foine thirsty, healthy corpse I am,' says I."

A dozen hands stretched out to give Kilquhanity a drink, for even the best story-teller of Pontiac could not have told his tale so well.

Yet the success achieved by Kilquhanity at such moments was discounted through long months of mingled suspicion and doubtful tolerance. Although both he and his wife were Catholics (so they said, and so it seemed), Kilquhanity never went to Confession or took the Blessed Sacrament. The Curé spoke to Kilquhanity's wife about it, and she said she could do nothing with her husband. Her tongue once loosed, she spoke freely, and what she said was little to the credit of Kilquhanity. Not that she could urge any horrible things against him; but she railed at minor faults till the Curé dismissed her with some good advice upon wives rehearsing their husband's faults, even to the parish priest.

Mrs. Kilquhanity could not get the Curé to listen to her, but she was more successful elsewhere. One day she came to get Kilquhanity's pension, which was sent every three months through

M. Garon, the Avocat. After she had handed over the receipt prepared beforehand by Kilquhanity, she replied to M. Garon's inquiry concerning her husband in these words: "Misther Garon, sir, such a man it is—enough to break the heart of anny woman. And the timper of him—Misther Garon, the timper of him's that awful, awful! No conshideration, and that ugly-hearted, got whin a soldier b'y! The things he does—my, my, the things he does!" She threw up her hands with an air of distraction.

"Well, and what does he do, Madame?" asked the Avocat simply.

"An' what he says, too—the awful of it! Ah, the bad sour heart in him! What's he lyin' in his bed for now—an' the New Year comin' on, whin we ought to be praisin' God an' enjoyin' each other's company in this blessed wurruld? What's he lying betune the quilts now fur, but by token of the bad heart in him! It's a wicked could he has, an' how did he come by it? I'll tell ye, Misther Garon. So wild was he, yesterday it was a week, so black mad wid somethin' I'd said to him and somethin' that shlipped from me hand at his head, that he turns his back on me, throws opin the dure, shteps out into the shnow, and shtandin' there alone, he curses the wide wurruld—oh, dear Misther Garon, he cursed the wide wurruld, shtandin' there in the snow! God forgive the black heart of him, shtandin' out there cursin' the wide wurruld!"

The Avocat looked at the Sergeant's wife musingly, the fingers of his hands tapping together, but he did not speak: he was becoming wiser all in a moment as to the ways of women.

"An' now he's in bed, the shtrappin' blasphemer, fur the could he got shtandin' there in the snow cursin' the wide wurruld. Ah, Misther Garon, pity a poor woman that has to live wid the loikes o' that!"

The Avocat still did not speak. He turned his face away and looked out of the window, where his eyes could see the little house on the hill, which to-day had the Union Jack flying in honour of some battle or victory, dear to Kilquhanity's heart. It looked peaceful enough, the little house lying there in the waste of snow, banked up with earth, and sheltered on the northwest by a little grove of pines. At last M. Garon rose, and lifting himself up and down on his toes as if about to deliver a legal opinion, he coughed slightly, and then said in a dry little voice:

"Madame, I shall have pleasure in calling on your husband. You have not seen the matter in the true light. Madame, I bid you good-day."

That night the Avocat, true to his promise, called on Sergeant Kilquhanity. Kilquhanity was alone in the house. His wife had gone to the village for the Little Chemist. She had been roused at last to the serious nature of Kilquhanity's illness.

M. Garon knocked. There was no answer. He knocked again more loudly, and still no answer. He opened the door and entered into a clean, warm living-room, so hot that the heat came to him in waves, buffeting his face. Dining, sitting, and drawing-room, it was also a sort of winter kitchen; and side by side with relics of Kilquhanity's soldier-life were clean, bright tins, black saucepans, strings of dried fruit, and well-cured hams. Certainly the place had the air of home; it spoke for the absent termagant.

M. Garon looked round and saw a half-opened door, through which presently came a voice speaking in a laboured whisper. The Avocat knocked gently at the door. "May I come in, Sergeant?" he

asked, and entered. There was no light in the room, but the fire in
the kitchen stove threw a glow over the bed where the sick man lay.
The big hands of the soldier moved restlessly on the quilt.

"Aw, it's the koind av ye!" said Kilquhanity, with difficulty, out of
the half shadows.

The Avocat took one burning hand in both of his, held it for a
moment, and pressed it two or three times. He did not know what to
say.

"We must have a light," said he at last, and taking a candle from
the shelf he lighted it at the stove and came into the bedroom again.
This time he was startled. Even in this short illness, Kilquhanity's
flesh had dropped away from him, leaving him but a bundle of
bones, on which the skin quivered with fever. Every word the sick
man tried to speak cut his chest like a knife, and his eyes half started
from his head with the agony of it. The Avocat's heart sank within
him, for he saw that a life was hanging in the balance. Not knowing
what to do, he tucked in the bedclothes gently.

"I do be thinkin'," said the strained, whispering voice—"I do be
thinkin' I could shmoke."

The Avocat looked round the room, saw the pipe on the
window, and cutting some tobacco from a "plug," he tenderly filled
the old black corn-cob. Then he put the stem in Kilquhanity's mouth
and held the candle to the bowl. Kilquhanity smiled, drew a long
breath, and blew out a cloud of thick smoke. For a moment he
puffed vigorously, then, all at once, the pleasure of it seemed to die
away, and presently the bowl dropped down on his chin. M. Garon
lifted it away. Kilquhanity did not speak, but kept saying something
over and over again to himself, looking beyond M. Garon
abstractedly.

At that moment the front door of the house opened, and presently a shrill voice came through the door: "Shmokin', shmokin', are ye, Kilquhanity? As soon as me back's turned, it's playin' the fool—" She stopped short, seeing the Avocat.

"Beggin' yer pardon, Misther Garon," she said, "I thought it was only Kilquhanity here, an' he wid no more sense than a babby."

Kilquhanity's eyes closed, and he buried one side of his head in the pillow, that her shrill voice should not pierce his ears.

"The Little Chemist'll be comin' in a minit, dear Misther Garon," said the wife presently, and she began to fuss with the bedclothes and to be nervously and uselessly busy.

"Aw, lave thim alone, darlin'," whispered Kilquhanity, tossing. Her officiousness seemed to hurt him more than the pain in his chest.

M. Garon did not wait for the Little Chemist to arrive, but after pressing the Sergeant's hand he left the house and went straight to the house of the Curé, and told him in what condition was the black sheep of his flock.

When M. Garon returned to his own home he found a visitor in his library. It was a woman, between forty and fifty years of age, who rose slowly to her feet as the Avocat entered, and, without preliminary, put into his hands a document.

"That is who I am," she said. "Mary Muddock that was, Mary Kilquhanity that is."

The Avocat held in his hands the marriage lines of Matthew Kilquhanity of the parish of Malahide and Mary Muddock of the parish of St. Giles, London. The Avocat was completely taken aback. He blew nervously through his pale fingers, raised himself up and down on his toes, and grew pale through suppressed excitement. He examined the certificate carefully, though from the first he had no doubt of its accuracy and correctness.

"Well?" said the woman, with a hard look in her face and a hard note in her voice. "Well?"

The Avocat looked at her musingly for a moment. All at once there had been unfolded to him Kilquhanity's story. In his younger days Kilquhanity had married this woman with a face of tin and a heart of leather. It needed no confession from Kilquhanity's own lips to explain by what hard paths he had come to the reckless hour when, at Blackpool, he had left her for ever, as he thought. In the flush of his criminal freedom he had married again—with the woman who shared his home on the little hillside, behind the Parish Church, she believing him a widower. Mary Muddock, with the stupidity of her class, had never gone to the right quarters to discover his whereabouts until a year before this day when she stood in the Avocat's library. At last, through the War Office, she had found the whereabouts of her missing Matthew. She had gathered her little savings together, and, after due preparation, had sailed away to Canada to find the soldier boy whom she had never given anything but bad hours in all the days of his life with her.

"Well," said the woman, "you're a lawyer—have you nothing to say? You pay his pension—next time you'll pay it to me. I'll teach him to leave me and my kid and go off with an Irish cook!"

The Avocat looked her steadily in the eyes, and then delivered the strongest blow that was possible from the opposite side of the case. "Madame," said he, "Madame, I regret to inform you that Matthew Kilquhanity is dying."

"Dying, is he?" said the woman, with a sudden change of voice and manner, but her whine did not ring true. "The poor darlin', and only that Irish hag to care for him! Has he made a will?" she added eagerly.

Kilquhanity had made no will, and the little house on the hillside, and all that he had, belonged to this woman who had spoiled the first part of his life, and had come now to spoil the last part.

An hour later the Avocat, the Curé, and the two women stood in the chief room of the little house on the hillside. The door was shut between the two rooms, and the Little Chemist was with Kilquhanity. The Curé's hand was on the arm of the first wife and the Avocat's upon the arm of the second. The two women were glaring eye to eye, having just finished as fine a torrent of abuse of each other and of Kilquhanity as can be imagined. Kilquhanity himself, with the sorrow of death upon him, though he knew it not, had listened to the brawl, his chickens come home to roost at last. The first Mrs. Kilquhanity had sworn, with an oath that took no account of the Curé's presence, that not a stick nor a stone nor a rag nor a penny should that Irish slattern have of Matthew Kilquhanity's!

The Curé and the Avocat had quieted them at last, and the Curé spoke sternly now to both women.

"In the presence of death," said he, "have done with your sinful clatter. Stop quarrelling over a dying man. Let him go in peace—let him go in peace! If I hear one word more," he added sternly, "I will turn you both out of the house into the night. I will have the man die in peace."

Opening the door of the bedroom, the Curé went in and shut the door, bolting it quietly behind him. The Little Chemist sat by the bedside, and Kilquhanity lay as still as a babe upon the bed. His eyes were half closed, for the Little Chemist had given him an opiate to quiet the terrible pain.

The Curé saw that the end was near. He touched Kilquhanity's arm: "My son," said he, "look up. You have sinned; you must confess your sins, and repent."

Kilquhanity looked up at him with dazed but half smiling eyes. "Are they gone? Are the women gone?" The Curé nodded his head. Kilquhanity's eyes closed and opened again. "They're gone, thin! Oh, the foine of it, the foine of it!" he whispered. "So quiet, so aisy, so quiet! Faith, I'll just be shlaping! I'll be shlaping now."

His eyes closed, but the Curé touched his arm again. "My son," said he, "look up. Do you thoroughly and earnestly repent you of your sins?"

His eyes opened again. "Yis, father, oh yis! There's been a dale o' noise—there's been a dale o' noise in the wurruld, father," said he. "Oh, so quiet, so quiet now! I do be shlaping."

A smile came upon his face. "Oh, the foine of it! I do be shlaping-shlaping."

And he fell into a noiseless Sleep.

THE BARON OF
BEAUGARD

66 The Manor House at Beaugard, monsieur? Ah, certainlee, I mind it very well. It was the first in Quebec, and there are many tales. It had a chapel and a gallows. Its baron, he had the power of life and death, and the right of the seigneur—you understand?—which he used only once; and then what trouble it made for him and the woman, and the barony, and the parish, and all the country!"

"What is the whole story, Larue?" said Medallion, who had spent months in the seigneur's company, stalking game, and tales, and legends of the St. Lawrence.

Larue spoke English very well—his mother was English.

"*Mais*, I do not know for sure; but the Abbé Frontone, he and I were snowed up together in that same house which now belongs to the Church, and in the big fireplace, where we sat on a bench, toasting our knees and our bacon, he told me the tale as he knew it. He was a great scholar—there is none greater. He had found papers in the wall of the house, and from the Gover'ment chest he got more. Then there were the tales handed down, and the records of the Church—for she knows the true story of every man that has come to New France from first to last. So, because I have a taste for tales, and gave him some, he told me of the Baron of Beaugard, and that time he took the right of the seigneur, and the end of it all.

"Of course it was a hundred and fifty years ago, when Bigot was Intendant—ah, what a rascal was that Bigot, robber and deceiver! He never stood by a friend, and never fought fair a foe—so the Abbé said. Well, Beaugard was no longer young. He had built the Manor House, he had put up his gallows, he had his vassals, he had been made a lord. He had quarrelled with Bigot, and had conquered, but at great cost; for Bigot had such power, and the Governor had trouble enough to care for himself against Bigot, though he was Beaugard's friend.

"Well, there was a good lump of a fellow who had been a soldier, and he picked out a girl in the Seigneury of Beaugard to make his wife. It is said the girl herself was not set for the man, for she was of finer stuff than the peasants about her, and showed it. But her father and mother had a dozen other children, and what was this girl, this Falise, to do? She said yes to the man, the time was fixed for the marriage, and it came along.

"So. At the very hour of the wedding Beaugard came by, for, the church was in mending, and he had given leave it should be in his own chapel. Well, he rode by just as the bride was coming out with the man—Garoche. When Beaugard saw Falise, he gave a whistle, then spoke in his throat, reined up his horse, and got down. He fastened his eyes on the girl's. A strange look passed between them— he had never seen her before, but she had seen him often, and when he was gone had helped the housekeeper with his rooms. She had carried away with her a stray glove of his. Of course it sounds droll, and they said of her when all came out that it was wicked; but evil is according to a man's own heart, and the girl had hid this glove as she hid whatever was in her soul—hid it even from the priest.

"Well, the Baron looked and she looked, and he took off his hat, stepped forward, and kissed her on the cheek. She turned pale as a ghost, and her eyes took the colour that her cheeks lost. When he stepped back he looked close at the husband. 'What is your name?' he said. 'Garoche, M'sieu' le Baron,' was the reply. 'Garoche, Garoche,' he said, eyeing him up and down. 'You have been a soldier?' 'Yes, M'sieu' le Baron.' 'You have served with me?' 'Against you, M'sieu' le Baron . . . when Bigot came fighting.' 'Better against me than for me,' said the Baron, speaking to himself, though he had so strong a voice that what he said could be heard by those near him—that is, those who were tall, for he was six and a half feet, with legs and shoulders like a bull.

"He stooped and stroked the head of his hound for a moment, and all the people stood and watched him, wondering what next. At last he said: 'And what part played you in that siege, Garoche?' Garoche looked troubled, but answered: 'It was in the way of duty, M'sieu' le Baron—I with five others captured the relief-party sent from your cousin the Seigneur of Vadrome.' 'Oh,' said the Baron, looking sharp, 'you were in that, were you? Then you know what happened to the young Marmette?' Garoche trembled a little, but drew himself up and said: 'M'sieu' le Baron, he tried to kill the Intendant—there was no other way.' 'What part played you in that, Garoche?' Some trembled, for they knew the truth, and they feared the mad will of the Baron. 'I ordered the firing-party, M'sieu' le Baron,' he answered.

"The Baron's eyes got fierce and his face hardened, but he stooped and drew the ears of the hound through his hand softly. 'Marmette was my cousin's son, and had lived with me,' he said. 'A brave lad, and he had a nice hatred of vileness—else he had not died.' A strange smile played on his lips for a moment, then he looked at Falise steadily. Who can tell what was working in his mind! 'War is war,' he went on, 'and Bigot was your master, Garoche; but the man pays for his master's sins this way or that. Yet I would not have it different, no, not a jot.' Then he turned round to the crowd, raised his hat to the Curé, who stood on the chapel steps, once more looked steadily at Falise, and said: 'You shall all come to the Manor House, and have your feastings there, and we will drink to the home-coming of the fairest woman in my barony.' With that he turned round, bowed to Falise, put on his hat, caught the bridle through his arm, and led his horse to the Manor House.

"This was in the afternoon. Of course, whether they wished or not, Garoche and Falise could not refuse, and the people were glad enough, for they would have a free hand at meat and wine, the Baron being liberal of table. And it was as they guessed, for though the time was so short, the people at Beaugard soon had the tables heavy with food and drink. It was just at the time of candle-lighting the Baron came in and gave a toast. 'To the dwellers in Eden to-night,' he said—'Eden against the time of the Angel and the Sword.' I do not think that any except the Curé and the woman understood, and she, maybe, only because a woman feels the truth about a thing, even when her brain does not. After they had done shouting to his toast, he said a good-night to all, and they began to leave, the Curé among the first to go, with a troubled look in his face.

"As the people left, the Baron said to Garoche and Falise: 'A moment with me before you go.' The woman started, for she thought of one thing, and Garoche started, for he thought of another—the siege of Beaugard and the killing of young Marmette. But they followed the Baron to his chamber. Coming in, he shut the door on them. Then he turned to Garoche. 'You will accept the roof and bed of Beaugard to-night, my man,' he said, 'and come to me here at nine tomorrow morning.' Garoche stared hard for an instant. 'Stay here!' said Garoche, 'Falise and me stay here in the Manor, M'sieu' le Baron!' 'Here, even here, Garoche; so good-night to you,' said the Baron. Garoche turned towards the girl. 'Then come, Falise,' he said, and reached out his hand. 'Your room, Garoche, shall be shown you at once,' the Baron added softly, 'the lady's at her pleasure.'

"Then a cry burst from Garoche, and he sprang forward, but the Baron waved him back. 'Stand off,' he said, 'and let the lady choose between us.' 'She is my wife,' said Garoche. 'I am your Seigneur,' said the other. 'And there is more than that,' he went on; 'for, damn me, she is too fine stuff for you, and the Church shall untie what she has tied to-day!' At that Falise fainted, and the Baron caught her as she fell. He laid her on a couch, keeping an eye on Garoche the while. 'Loose her gown,' he said, 'while I get brandy.' Then he turned to a cupboard, poured liquor, and came over. Garoche had her dress open at the neck and bosom, and was staring at something on her breast. The Baron saw also, stooped with a strange sound in his throat, and picked it up. 'My glove!' he said. 'And on her wedding-day!' He pointed. 'There on the table is its mate, fished this morning from my hunting-coat—a pair the Governor gave me. You see, man, you see her choice!'

"At that he stooped and put some brandy to her lips. Garoche drew back sick and numb, and did nothing, only stared. Falise came to herself soon, and when she felt her dress open, gave a cry. Garoche could have killed her then, when he saw her shudder from him, as if afraid, over towards the Baron, who held the glove in his hand, and said: 'See, Garoche, you had better go. In the next room they will tell you where to sleep. To-morrow, as I said, you will meet me here. We shall have things to say, you and I.' Ah, that Baron, he had a queer mind, but in truth he loved the woman, as you shall see!

"Garoche got up without a word, went to the door and opened it, the look of the Baron and the woman following him, for there was a devil in his eye. In the other room there were men waiting, and he was taken to a chamber and locked in. You can guess what that night must have been to him!"

"What was it to the Baron and Falise?" asked Medallion.

"M'sieu', what do you think? Beaugard had never had an eye for women; loving his hounds, fighting, quarrelling, doing wild, strong things. So, all at once, he was face to face with a woman who has the look of love in her face, who was young, and fine of body—so the Abbe said—and was walking to marriage at her father's will and against her own, carrying the Baron's glove in her bosom. What should Beaugard do? But no, ah no, m'sieu', not as you think, not quite! Wild, with the bit in his teeth, yes; but at heart—well, here was the one woman for him. He knew it all in a minute, and he would have her once and for all, and till death should come their way. And so he said to her, as he raised her, she drawing back afraid, her heart hungering for him, yet fear in her eyes, and her fingers trembling as she softly pushed him from her. You see, she did not know quite what was in his heart. She was the daughter of a tenant vassal, who had lived in the family of a grand seigneur in her youth, the friend of his child—that was all, and that was where she got her manners and her mind.

"She got on her feet and said: 'M'sieu' le Baron, you will let me go—to my husband. I cannot stay here. Oh, you are great, you are noble, you would not make me sorry, make me to hate myself—and you! I have only one thing in the world of any price—you would not steal my happiness?' He looked at her steadily in the eyes, and said: 'Will it make you happy to go to Garoche?' She raised her hands and wrung them. 'God knows, God knows, I am his wife,' she said helplessly, 'and he loves me.' 'And God knows, God knows,' said the Baron, 'it is all a question of whether one shall feed and two go hungry, or two gather and one have the stubble! Shall not he stand in the stubble? What has he done to merit you?

"What would he do? You are for the master, not the man; for love, not the feeding on; for the Manor House and the hunt, not the cottage and the loom.'

"She broke into tears, her heart thumping in her throat. 'I am for what the Church did for me this day,' she said. 'O sir, I pray you, forgive me and let me go. Do not punish me, but forgive me—and let me go. I was wicked to wear your glove—wicked, wicked.' 'But no,' was his reply, 'I shall not forgive you so good a deed, and you shall not go. And what the Church did for you this day she shall undo—by all the saints, she shall! You came sailing into my heart this hour past on a strong wind, and you shall not slide out on an ebb-tide. I have you here, as your Seigneur, but I have you here as a man who will—'

"He sat down by her at that point, and whispered softly in her ear; at which she gave a cry which had both gladness and pain. 'Surely, even that,' he said, catching her to his breast. 'And the Baron of Beaugard never broke his word.' What should be her reply? Does not a woman when she truly loves always believe? That is the great sign. She slid to her knees and dropped her head into the hollow of his arm. 'I do not understand these things,' she said, 'but I know that the other was death, and this is life. And yet I know, too, for my heart says so, that the end—the end, will be death.'

"'Tut, tut, my flower, my wild-rose!' he said. 'Of course the end of all is death, but we will go a-Maying first, come October, and let the world break over us when it must. We are for Maying now, my rose of all the world!' It was as if he meant more than he said, as if he saw what would come in that October which all New France never forgot, when, as he said, the world broke over them.

"The next morning the Baron called Garoche to him. The man was like some mad buck harried by the hounds, and he gnashed his teeth behind his shut lips. The Baron eyed him curiously, yet kindly, too, as well he might, for when was ever man to hear such a speech as came to Garoche the morning after his marriage? 'Garoche,' the Baron said, having waved his men away, 'as you see, the lady made her choice—and for ever. You and she have said your last farewell in this world—for the wife of the Baron of Beaugard can have nothing to say to Garoche the soldier.' At that Garoche snarled out, 'The wife of the Baron of Beaugard, that is a lie to shame all hell.' The Baron wound the lash of a riding-whip round and round his fingers quietly and said: 'It is no lie, my man, but the truth.' Garoche eyed him savagely, and growled: 'The Church made her my wife yesterday; and you—you—you—ah, you who had all—you with your money and place, which could get all easy, you take the one thing I have! You, the grand seigneur, are only a common robber! Ah, Jésu—if you would but fight me!'

"The Baron, very calm, said: 'First, Garoche, the lady was only your wife by a form which the Church shall set aside—it could never have been a true marriage. Second, it is no stealing to take from you what you did not have. I took what was mine—remember the glove! For the rest—to fight you? No, my churl, you know that's impossible. You may shoot me from behind a tree or a rock, but swording with you—come, come, a pretty gossip for the Court! Then, why wish a fight? Where would you be, as you stood before me—you!' The Baron stretched himself up, and smiled down at Garoche. 'You have your life, man; take it and go—to the farthest corner of New France, and show not your face here again. If I find you ever again in Beaugard I will have you whipped from parish to parish. Here is money for you—good gold coins. Take them, and go.'

"Garoche got still and cold as stone. He said in a low, harsh voice: 'M'sieu' le Baron, you are a common thief, a wolf, a snake. Such men as you come lower than Judas. As God has an eye to see, you shall pay all one day. I do not fear you nor your men nor your gallows. You are a jackal, and the woman has a filthy heart—a ditch of shame.'

"The Baron drew up his arm like lightning, and the lash of his whip came singing across Garoche's pale face. Where it passed, a red welt rose, but the man never stirred. The arm came up again, but a voice' behind the Baron said: 'Ah no, no, not again!' There stood Falise. Both men looked at her. 'I have heard Garoche,' she said. 'He does not judge me right. My heart is no filthy ditch of shame; but it was breaking when I came from the altar with him yesterday. Yet I would have been a true wife to him after all. A ditch of shame—ah, Garoche—Garoche! And you said you loved me, and that nothing could change you!'

"The Baron said to her: 'Why have you come, Falise? I forbade you.' 'Oh, my lord,' she answered, 'I feared—for you both! When men go mad because of women a devil enters into them.' The Baron, taking her by the hand, said: 'Permit me,' and he led her to the door for her to pass out. She looked back sadly at Garoche, standing for a minute very still. Then Garoche said: 'I command you, come with me; you are my wife.' She did not reply, but shook her head at him. Then he spoke out high and fierce: 'May no child be born to you. May a curse fall on you. May your fields be barren, and your horses and cattle die. May you never see nor hear good things. May the waters leave their courses to drown you, and the hills their bases to bury you, and no hand lay you in decent graves!'

"The woman put her hands to her ears and gave a little cry, and the Baron pushed her gently on, and closed the door after her. Then he turned on Garoche. 'Have you said all you wish?' he asked. 'For, if not, say on, and then go; and go so far you cannot see the sky that covers Beaugard. We are even now—we can cry quits. But that I have a little injured you, you should be done for instantly. But hear me: if I ever see you again, my gallows shall end you straight. Your tongue has been gross before the mistress of this Manor; I will have it torn out if it so much as syllables her name to me or to the world again. She is dead to you. Go, and go for ever!'

"He put a bag of money on the table, but Garoche turned away from it, and without a word left the room, and the house, and the parish, and said nothing to any man of the evil that had come to him.

"But what talk was there, and what dreadful things were said at first—that Garoche had sold his wife to the Baron; that he had been killed and his wife taken; that the Baron kept him a prisoner in a cellar under the Manor House! And all the time there was Falise with the Baron—very quiet and sweet and fine to see, and going to Chapel every day, and to Mass on Sundays—which no one could understand, any more than they could see why she should be called the Baroness of Beaugard; for had they all not seen her married to Garoche? And there were many people who thought her vile. Yet truly, at heart, she was not so—not at all. Then it was said that there was to be a new marriage; that the Church would let it be so, doing and undoing, and doing again. But the weeks and the months went by, and it was never done. For, powerful as the Baron was, Bigot the Intendant was powerful also, and fought the thing with all his might. The Baron went to Quebec to see the Bishop and the Governor, and though promises were made, nothing was done. It must go to the King and then to the Pope, and from the Pope to the King again, and so on. And the months and the years went by as they waited, and with them came no child to the Manor House of Beaugard. That was the only sad thing—that and the waiting, so far as man could see. For never were man and woman truer to each other than these, and never was a lady of the Manor kinder to the poor, or a lord freer of hand to his vassals. He would bluster sometimes, and string a peasant up by the heels, but his gallows was never used; and, what was much in the minds of the people, the Curé did not refuse the woman the sacrament.

"At last the Baron, fierce because he knew that Bigot was the cause of the great delay, so that he might not call Falise his wife, seized a transport on the river, which had been sent to brutally levy upon a poor gentleman, and when Bigot's men resisted, shot them down. Then Bigot sent against Beaugard a company of artillery and some soldiers of the line. The guns were placed on a hill looking down on the Manor House across the little river. In the evening the cannons arrived, and in the morning the fight was to begin. The guns were loaded and everything was ready. At the Manor all was making ready also, and the Baron had no fear.

"But Falise's heart was heavy, she knew not why. 'Eugene,' she said, 'if anything should happen!' 'Nonsense, my Falise,' he answered; 'what should happen?' 'If—if you were taken—were killed!' she said. 'Nonsense, my rose,' he said again, 'I shall not be killed. But if I were, you should be at peace here.' 'Ah, no, no!' said she. 'Never. Life to me is only possible with you. I have had nothing but you—none of those things which give peace to other women—none. But I have been happy—yes, very happy. And, God forgive me, Eugene, I cannot regret, and I never have! But it has been always and always my prayer that, when you die, I may die with you—at the same moment. For I cannot live without you, and, besides, I would like to go to the good God with you to speak for us both; for oh, I loved you, I loved you, and I love you still, my husband, my adored!'

"He stooped—he was so big, and she but of middle height—kissed her, and said: 'See, my Falise, I am of the same mind. We have been happy in life, and we could well be happy in death together.' So they sat long, long into the night and talked to each other—of the days they had passed together, of cheerful things, she trying to comfort herself, and he trying to bring smiles to her lips. At last they said good-night, and he lay down in his clothes; and after a few moments she was sleeping like a child. But he could not sleep, for he lay thinking of her and of her life—how she had come from humble things and fitted in with the highest. At last, at break of day, he arose and went outside. He looked up at the hill where Bigot's two guns were. Men were already stirring there. One man was standing beside the gun, and another not far behind. Of course the Baron could not know that the man behind the gunner said: 'Yes, you may open the dance with an early salute'; and he smiled up boldly at the hill and went into the house, and stole to the bed of his wife to kiss her before he began the day's fighting. He looked at her a moment, standing over her, and then stooped and softly put his lips to hers.

"At that moment the gunner up on the hill used the match, and an awful thing happened. With the loud roar the whole hillside of rock and gravel and sand split down, not ten feet in front of the gun, moved with horrible swiftness upon the river, filled its bed, turned it from its course, and, sweeping on, swallowed the Manor House of Beaugard. There had been a crack in the hill, the water of the river had sapped its foundations, and it needed only this shock to send it down.

"And so, as the woman wished: the same hour for herself and the man! And when at last their prison was opened by the hands of Bigot's men, they were found cheek by cheek, bound in the sacred marriage of Death.

"But another had gone the same road, for, at the awful moment, beside the bursted gun, the dying gunner, Garoche, lifted up his head, saw the loose travelling hill, and said with his last breath: 'The waters drown them, and the hills bury them, and—'

"He had his way with them, and after that perhaps the great God had His way with him—perhaps."

A Note on the Text
and the Author

The Lane That Had No Turning was published in New York by Doubleday, Page & Co. in 1900. The Canadian edition (published by George N. Morang) and British edition (published by Heineman) were published the same year and appear to be printed from the same plates.

Gilbert Parker—in full, Horatio Gilbert George Parker—had been born in Camden East in what is now the province of Ontario in 1862. He travelled widely as a young man and became established in the UK as a writer in the final decade of the nineteenth century. The first four stories of those that comprise *The Lane That Had No Turning* were published in *The Illustrated London News* in 1892. Parker later declared that he "had perhaps greater joy in writing them . . . than in almost anything else I have written."

Omitted from this edition are nine short fantasies that were grouped under the umbrella title "Parables of a Province." Described by Parker as being "more or less mystical in nature," they differ in style from the other stories in the book and Parkert himself admitted they were not popular; in fact, he had difficulty in securing magazine publication of the "parables" in the United States or Britain.

Parker was one of the most popular Canadian writers of his era, with his books becoming best-sellers in the United States. He was knighted for his contributions to Canadian literature in 1902. Parker served as a member of the British Parliament from 1900 to 1918. An advocate of closer ties among the colonies and dominions of the Empire and the mother country, he was tasked during the First World War with propaganda and publicity work aimed at drawing the United States over to the Allied cause.

Parker died in 1932.

Milestones in Canadian Literature

This series is designed to bring intriguing and important works of Canadian literature back into print so that they can provide enjoyment and illumination to new generations of readers. Books in the series are re-published in handsome new editions, with the type completely re-set, with errors in the earlier editions corrected, and with new introductions, notes, and commentary provided that serve to place the books in a contemporary context.

www.ingramcontent.com/pod-product-compliance
Lightning Source LLC
Chambersburg PA
CBHW071817020726
47502CB00004B/1140